PLEASE SIR!

The Official History

ACORN BOOKS

David Barry

Foreword by Peter Cleall

Published in 2020 by
Acorn Books
www.acornbooks.co.uk

Copyright © 2020 David Barry

The right of David Barry to be identified
as the author of this work has been asserted
by him in accordance with the Copyright,
Designs and Patents Act 1988.

The opinions expressed herein belong to
the author and do not necessarily reflect those
of Acorn Books or Andrews UK Limited.

Contents

To all my *Please Sir!* friends
and colleagues, past and present

Acknowledgements

I am deeply indebted to Kevin Cann who proof-read the book and edited it brilliantly. His questions about certain events induced me to add more material, and his comments and suggestions were always knowledgeable. Not only that but the process was hugely enjoyable, and I am extremely grateful for his invaluable help, and also for the laughs we shared along the way.

I would also like to thank publisher Paul Andrews of Andrews UK for giving me the opportunity of sharing this autobiographical story of one of television's greatest hits, and of the many actors, directors and writers involved in its creation.

Thanks also to everyone at Andrews UK, especially Joe Larkins for his technical wizardry and help in putting all this together.

Foreword

David Barry has a long history in the 'business of show'. He has worked successfully as an actor, director, producer and latterly as a writer. Here he has written an entertaining and informative story of his progress through the jungle of entertainment with the definitive account of the evolution of *Please Sir!* at its core.

The pages are filled with amusing anecdotes about his encounters with actors and directors. Household names are sprinkled throughout and many a reputation hits the dust.

I enjoyed working with David on *Please Sir!* and on a variety of projects since and have appreciated his friendship throughout the last fifty years.

Peter Cleall

Introduction

When I began working on *Please Sir!* I had been an actor for over twelve years, having performed my first professional role at the age of 12, since I attended Corona Academy, a stage school in west London. In those early teenage years, I worked with actors like Tyrone Power, Mai Zetterling, Paul Scofield, Laurence Olivier and Vivien Leigh, all of whom knew me by my real name of Meurig Wyn-Jones. So why, in the mid-sixties, did I change my name?

It was at the suggestion of an older actor who pointed out that if I attended auditions, and with a name like mine, directors would expect to meet a young actor with a pronounced Welsh accent, not with the homogenized English way of speaking I had been forced to adopt during my first year at stage school; because in 1955, kitchen sink dramas had yet to become part of the theatrical scene and regional dialects were not yet de rigeur.

My journey as David Barry began with eight episodes of the five evenings a week soap opera *Crossroads*, but the least said about that, the better. I consider that to be a false start, not even a learning curve. And so, my far more fun and stimulating odyssey began in 1968, and it was an adventure that lasted far longer than I would ever have guessed.

I would like to take you with me on that trip, which I hope you will enjoy as much as I did. Of course, no journey is without its setbacks, and there have been many pratfalls along the way as you will discover as you read on.

But before taking that first step, I would like to give you a health warning, as I wouldn't want to cause offence. You will encounter some strong language in the book, because I have described as accurately as possible the way some actors behave. I could have inserted asterisks into certain letters of swear words, but as your mind could fill in the gaps I thought this might be patronizing, and decided it was best to tell it as it is.

Despite some bad language, my aim is to entertain you with a behind-the-scenes view of what it was really like to work in a hit television series, a series that refuses to die and is still going strong after more than 50 years. And as a middle-aged man told me recently, he has fond memories of being taken when he was five-years-old by an older sibling to see the *Please Sir!* film when it was first released and gave him a lifelong love of film and television comedy.

And I guess, dear reader, that you already have a love of television comedy, otherwise you wouldn't have bought this book. So go on, enjoy it!

David Barry
October 2020

PLEASE SIR!

The Official History

Back to School

For me, the sixties was a wonderfully childish decade. Not just because soup tins had become works of art, and Yoko Ono had made a film about naked buttocks and not much else, but mainly because I was about to start school again at the age of 25.

I nearly didn't get to sit behind that desk, though, because early that year I auditioned for the hippie, draft-dodging musical *Hair,* and the anonymous producers in the darkened auditorium loved my audition. There had been so much publicity about the show and its New York success, I knew exactly how to dress the part: shirt hanging out of torn flared denims, and a waistcoat made of what looked like an old carpet, and flip-flops on my feet. At least my attempts to look like an actor who knew what the show was about seemed to go down well. Unlike the young actress who auditioned before me. She wore a cute party frock, and in her total ignorance of knowing what the show was about, she sang 'I Enjoy Being a Girl' from *Flower Drum Song.* I don't know how many bars into her song she got before they hooked her. 'Next!' Which was me, and I managed to get through to the end of my song, singing (angrily) an Irish rebel song, which ended with 'Fuck the British Army', followed by my gesture of a V-sign – not the Churchillian one for victory. They loved it, and I made the recall audition. The first audition I had treated light heartedly, not really expecting a great response and not caring whether it was sink or swim, but now I was recalled I began to take it seriously. Big mistake. I should really have given them the same song again at the next audition. Instead, I sang a Manfred Mann number: 'My Name is Jack'. I don't think they liked it as much as the Irish rebel song, and so that was that. Which was just as well, because a part in *Hair* would have meant the loss of the *Please Sir!* and *The Fenn Street Gang* series that ran between 1968 and 1973. Maybe my failed *Hair* audition was meant to be.

In the autumn I auditioned, along with about 30 other young actors for the series called *Rough House.* The auditions were held at Station House, the

1

head offices and rehearsal rooms of LWT, the television company not yet a year old, which had won the franchise from Associated Rediffusion, and would be transmitting from early evening on Fridays until late on Sundays. Station House was a 20-storey building near Stonebridge Park station, not far from Wembley and the studios which were used by London Weekend Television.

Mark Stuart, the producer and director, and the writers, John Esmonde and Bob Larbey, sat in front of a long table. We the actors waited in another room and then three of us were ushered in to stand before them and read from a script. As soon as I read for the part of Frankie Abbott, I shrugged my shoulders audaciously and imagined reaching for the semi-automatic pistol concealed under my arm. I saw John Esmonde laugh and tug his goatee beard, which I took to be a good sign.

Once we had read, we were sent back into the other room, and Mark Stuart's PA would enter at odd intervals, tap someone on the shoulder and say, 'Thank you. You can go.' Then three of us would go in again to read for Dunstable, Craven and Abbott, which were the parts they were casting that day. Whenever I had given my reading, I dreaded the P.A.'s dismissive tap on the shoulder. Eventually, after nail-biting minutes, three of us were left in the other room: Malcolm McFee, Peter Denyer and yours truly. Then Mark Stuart came in and announced with a twinkle in his eye, 'Well, I guess you three will have to do. We'll be in touch with your agents.'

The three of us caught the train at Stonebridge Park to return to central London. It was mid-afternoon, and we wondered if we would hear from our agents before the end of the day. We chatted amicably, Malcolm mentioned he had recently finished filming *Oh What a Lovely War*, playing one of the Smiths in the Richard Attenborough star-studded film. Peter and I had previously worked together the year before, and we reminisced about performing in *Zigger Zagger* a play about disenfranchised youth and football hooliganism, written by Peter Terson for the National Youth Theatre. West End producer Peter Bridge, responding to his son's love of the play and football, decided to mount a professional production, and it pretty much bankrupted him. The play had a cast of eighty, and every actor in the production was on a minimum Equity contract. Whether the public was not interested in the subject matter, or the play didn't satisfy their craving to see star names, whatever the reason the play opened to abysmal advance box office takings of only £34, which in today's money would be only equivalent to around £430. No wonder poor Peter Bridge, one of the loveliest producers ever, lost his shirt. It closed after only ten performances, and our first night drink's party became the last night's wake.

When I got home, I immediately phoned my agent, Keith Whitall, and told him I *thought* I had got the part, but he hadn't yet heard from LWT. 'Never mind, darling,' he said. 'I expect they'll be in touch tomorrow.'

I was married to Zélie in 1967, both of us having met a year before while working at Butlin's Repertory Theatre in Pwllheli, where we performed six plays a fortnight throughout the summer. It was always difficult finding a decent flat in London, so when we saw one advertised in the evening paper in the select area of Highgate Village, asking prospective tenants to ring after six, I dialled the number at five o'clock and patiently listened to the ring tone for a good hour before it was answered, but it meant I was first off the mark, and we moved into the small flat just a few doors from The Flask pub on Highgate West Hill. The flat cost us around £40.00 per month, which in today's money would be around £700 and to pay for it we both worked as messengers at J. Walter Thompson, one of the world's largest advertising agencies at that time, located in Berkeley Square.

Even though Mark Stuart had more or less told the three of us that we had got the job, I still suffered from the typical actor's insecurity as nothing had been confirmed yet, and I didn't know whether to celebrate or not, so Zélie and I spent the evening boozing in the lovely Highgate Village pubs, a sort of tentative, half-celebration. The phone call came the next day, offering four episodes, with an option for a further three. Rehearsals began a week later.

The first read-through was in a large rehearsal room at Station House, and it was exciting sitting around a large table listening to the actors playing the staff members. I didn't ever remember seeing John Alderton before, not having been fond of hospital soaps. He played Dr Moon in *Emergency Ward 10,* during which time he met his first wife, Jill Brown. It was, apparently, a single appearance in *Never A Cross Word,* a comedy series starring Paul Daneman and Nyree Dawn Porter, that led to him being cast as Bernard Hedges. Deryck Guyler, cast as Norman Potter, the school caretaker, and Noel Howlett, as Cromwell, the headmaster, I remembered from different episodes of *Hancock's Half Hour,* one of my all-time favourite shows, both on radio and television. Deryck was the policeman in the episode *The Radio Ham,* and Noel was a vicar in an episode when various BBC characters get stuck in one of the Broadcasting House lifts with Hancock. And I could recall the funny line of Tony Hancock's as Noel was about to press the button to summon the lift: 'Ah! The ecclesiastical digit.' Joan Sanderson (Miss Ewell) I recognised but couldn't recall what I had seen her in, and likewise Erik Chitty (Smithy). I recognised Richard Davies, though, from *Zulu,* who played Private 593 Jones, who has a memorable speech about the confusion of so many Joneses in the regiment. And during our read-through, Richard also had some hilarious and memorable lines as Mr Price, the most seen-it-all cynic in the staffroom.

Peter Denyer, I knew from the ill-fated *Zigger Zagger.* His character in the series was Dennis Dunstable, a special needs teenager, referred to in the scripts by the anachronistic 'educationally sub normal' epithet. And I had met Malcolm McFee at the auditions. His characterisation of Peter Craven, dapper and laid-back, with a pimp roll in his gait, was perfect casting. As were the other three I met on that first day of rehearsals: Peter Cleall, as Eric Duffy, the class leader, tough, rebellious and disobedient but with a soft heart; Penny Spencer as the sexy Sharon, who underneath it all was far from dumb; and one of my favourite characters, Maureen Bullock, played by Liz Gebhardt, who in later scripts would become F.A's tart (in his dreams), and in real life become a close friend of mine.

Frank Muir was LWT's Head of Entertainment, and he sat close to me during the read-through. I could hear him chuckling, and occasionally laughing loudly, which was encouraging. Most people recognised Frank Muir's very distinctive looks (he was a regular panellist on BBC TV's *Call My Bluff*). But it was his and his long-term partner Denis Norden's writing I was most familiar with. For years they had written *Take It from Here* for the radio, and *The Glums* segment was another comedy favourite of mine.

Following the read-through, it was coffee time, and a chance for the cast to get to know one another. Most of us were aware that there was a bit of a conflab going on between Frank Muir, Mark Stuart and Esmonde and Larbey. There were things to be ironed out in the script, and the title, *Rough House,* was a problem. However, after coffee we all began rehearsing, blocking the scenes in the makeshift set. There were six classroom desks for us, positioned where they would be in the studio, and Bernard Hedges' desk, raised on a three inch high rostrum.

The second day was a location shoot for the filmed insert, which was the start of the show, showing the pupils, including 5C, heading for Fenn Street School on a double-decker bus, which Bernard Hedges catches and finds himself sitting next to Eric Duffy. He has no idea that Eric is to be his 5C pupil and lights his fag for him. The harassed bus conductor was played by Bob Todd, an actor who began acting at the age of 42. He had, apparently, met scriptwriters Ray Galton and Alan Simpson in a pub, bluffed them into thinking he was an actor, and was given the part of a policeman in the Sid James comedy *Citizen James*. But we all recognised him as the actor from a Knorr Soup commercial.

On day three we were back in the rehearsal room, and the title was changed to *Please Sir!'* I can't remember the original ending to the first episode *The Welcome Mat*, but now in the story Hedges unwittingly gains a reputation as a karate expert. It was established that the classroom desk was rotten, and towards the end of the episode he enters the rowdy classroom and attempts to keep order by striking the worm-eaten desk, which is split in half by what the pupils think is his karate chop. The show went from a weak ending to a big finish and we wondered if this suggestion came from Frank Muir.

On the day of the first episode in Wembley Studios, all of us 5C actors had to go early to wardrobe and get into the costumes we would be wearing, so that we were in our costumes for the technical camera rehearsal, when everything runs very slowly as the crew deal with all the problems we might encounter prior to the dress rehearsal, which would be in the afternoon of the following day.

After I got kitted out in my combat jacket, I went into the studio to find John Alderton already sitting at his desk in the classroom, looking just like a young teacher fresh out of teacher training college, wearing a drab, brown tweedy jacket. I went up to him and said something like, 'That is a brilliant costume, John, just the sort of naff thing a young teacher would wear.'

By reply I got a funny look, as if I was winding him up.

Later on I discovered he hadn't yet been to wardrobe to get kitted out, and those were his own clothes!

Our studio floor manager for this first series was David Yallop who would go on to write many true crime books like *Deliver Us From Evil* about the Yorkshire Ripper, and *In God's Name* a conspiracy theory about the murder of Pope John Paul l.

When the dress rehearsal began for episode one, we heard the distinctive theme tune, which kicked off with a school bell ringing. This instrumental was composed by Sam Fonteyn and used for each series. It was called 'School's Out', and years later I wondered if Alice Cooper had appropriated the title for his worldwide hit single in 1972?

The first series got as high as nine in the ratings, playing to 6.8 million homes, and the options were taken up to do seven episodes. The episodes were 40 minutes long, for a 45-minute slot, broadcast in black and white, as colour television was nearly a year away from its launch.

On the twentieth floor of Station House was the canteen and bar, and in those days a boozy lunchtime was not frowned upon. Following a hasty meal, we invariably continued drinking in the bar, usually celebrating our jump into the ratings, although I don't think most of us needed an excuse to drink and socialise.

When I got to know Peter Cleall better, he told me he had appeared in *Crossroads* as a character called Chuck Feeney, and he said it was a heap of shit. I agreed with him, because four years previously I had appeared in eight episodes of this five nights a week soap, playing Ross Baxter. We both had a laugh as we imagined a television series starring Chuck Feeney and Ross Baxter, and envisaged scenes that were as naff as our *Crossroads* appearances.

It was great hearing the stories of the staff members of the cast. I remember Deryck Guyler telling us he did a voice over as a news broadcaster for the radio announcement in the long-running Agatha Christie West End play *The Mousetrap,* then in its fifth year, for which he received something like sixpence a week, and as there were forty sixpences to the pound, he would have earned one pound and six shillings annually. The change to decimal currency happened in 1971, so I guess it was adjusted. But what was so great about Deryck's royalty for *The* Mousetrap is that it has become a theatrical tradition. Writing this in early 2020, when *The Mousetrap* is in its 66th year, the production company informed me that it is still Deryck's voice over that is being used in the whodunit, and he hasn't missed a performance for almost 66 years, making him the longest serving cast member.

One of Deryck's most treasured memories he told us was when he worked in a West End show in 1945, and on 7 May, the day before the official VE Day celebrations, he was the performer who stopped the show, stepped forward with tears in his eyes and announced that Germany had surrendered and the war in Europe was over. The audience went berserk, he said.

Noel Howlett always greeted everyone with a bright 'good morning' whenever he arrived for rehearsals. When he was asked about his sunny greeting, he told us that when he worked as a young boy with Mrs Patrick Campbell, the renowned actress who knew and worked with George Bernard Shaw and was also a close friend of Oscar Wilde, Noel would always mumble 'good morning'. The actress took him aside one day and said, 'Mr Howlett, whenever you greet me with a downward inflection, I feel depressed for the rest of the day. Kindly greet me with an upward inflection in future.' Noel said it stayed with him the rest of his life, so that he always used an upward inflected greeting.

The furniture that was used in the rehearsal room was similar to the studio furniture but remained in the rehearsal room and was not transported to the studio each week. Our rehearsal classroom only needed six desks for us as the main characters. While Mark directed the staffroom scenes, we would either sit at the edges of the rehearsal room and watch, or we might remain at our desks until we were required to work on the next classroom scene. Often while we waited behind our desks, we passed the time by writing quietly in the prop exercise books. One time I can remember we made up anagrams of our names, and Malcolm McFee became Fecal Memmcol; Liz Gebhardt was Zebard Light; Peter Cleall changed to Leper Cleat; but my favourite was Peter Denyer who became Deeper Entry. Peter became slightly nettled by his anagrammed name and we wondered why. What none of us realized at the time was that Peter was gay, or perhaps he hadn't realized it himself at the time. It wasn't until a few years later when Malcolm and I were on tour and we visited Bournemouth where Peter was appearing in a summer season that he was open about his sexuality and seemed a great deal happier.

We very quickly became a great team and enjoyed working on the series. And this expanded time slot for what was usually half an hour, worked very well. And so many of John and Bob's lines were great. I especially used to love Price's cynicism, with wonderful lines like the ones in response to Hedges wanting 5C to join his chess club. 'If your lot join my chess club, be like inviting the Gestapo to a bar mitzvah.' Potter's malapropisms were a joy to listen to, and I can recall one of my own favourite lines in the final episode when we were about to break up for the Christmas holidays and Maureen and Sharon were reminiscing about a nativity play. Sharon said, 'Remember when we were first formers, Maur, and I was the Virgin Mary,' To which Abbott chips in, ''Bout the only year you could've been, weren't it?' Which barely got a laugh during the final run-through in the rehearsal room. This last rehearsal was always unnerving, because it was attended by the vision mixer, floor manager, cameramen and sound, and they were there to concentrate on the technical aspects of running the show, so our lines barely got noticed, everyone too busy listening to Mark pointing out various problems that might occur.

Mark's direction, we soon discovered, could be very basic. Once I asked him what my motivation was for a certain line, to which he replied, 'It's because you get fucking paid to say it.' And if any characters ended a scene with a visual shot, Mark's direction would be along the lines of, 'Come on, give me a mixed bag of reactions.'

7.30 PLEASE, SIR!
JOHN ALDERTON
DERYCK GUYLER
NOEL HOWLETT in
It's the Thought that Counts
BY JOHN ESMONDE AND BOB LARBEY
End-of-term at Fen Street, and the
staff wait for their traditional presents
from their forms.
Bernard's anticipation at the thoughts
of what he might get from 5C is
tempered by the news that the injured
Mr. Wiggins will be fit to return as
5C's form master next term.
When Miss Ewell takes a hand,
surprises are in store for Bernard
all round.

Bernard Hedges	John Alderton
Mr. Cromwell	Noel Howlett
Potter	Deryck Guyler
Price	Richard Davies
Smithy	Erik Chitty
Duffy	Peter Cleall
Craven	Malcolm McFee
Sharon Eversleigh	Penny Spencer
Maureen Bullock	Liz Gebhardt
Dunstable	Peter Denyer
Abbott	David Barry
Miss Ewell	Joan Sanderson
Barman	James Beattie

DESIGNER BARBARA BATES: PRODUCER/
DIRECTOR MARK STUART
London Weekend Television Production

The series was transmitted on Friday evenings at 8.30. Except episodes 4 & 5, *A Near Greek Tragedy* and *Barbarian Librarians*, these were transmitted at 9.15 as they contained a few swear words, though they were mild by today's standards.

Over the seven weeks and seven episodes, the time flew by, while everyone's characters were well established and expanded on, and London Weekend Television realized they had a hit on their hands. Although you would never have guessed it from their glossy photographs of all their shows in reception at Wembley Studios. There wasn't one of *Please Sir!* And it wasn't the cast members being paranoid. Whenever any of our wives, friends or agents came to a recording, they invariably noticed how our series was overlooked as far as the studio promotion went. But it was early days, and the series wasn't long established, even though it had taken off as far as the public was concerned.

But as we headed towards the last episode of the series, with the seven weeks zooming by with the blink of an eye, rumours went around that LWT would be recommissioning another series. As I loved working in this series, especially with a cast who got on so well and were already starting to feel like a family, I couldn't wait for the spring of the following year.

When is a Contract Not a Contract?

The last episode of the first series of *Please Sir!* was recorded and broadcast close to Christmas, and LWT, knowing they had a hit on their hands, quickly negotiated a further seven episodes to start in the spring. The contracts arrived early in the new year, and I thought this done deal meant the money from the first series might last until the new series began.

But none of us discerned that working for a big organisation like LWT was like swimming with sharks. On reflection, swimming with sharks might be less precarious or traumatic.

It wasn't long before our agents got a call from casting director Richard Price, saying that LWT wanted to make thirteen episodes but starting in the autumn. But, we all protested, what about the contracts we had already signed for the seven episodes starting in the spring? A done deal, surely? A contract is a contract and must be honoured. Not if we wanted to be cast in the longer series starting in the autumn. If I didn't tear up the seven-episode contract my agent was told, releasing LWT from having to honour it, then they would recast Frankie Abbott with another actor.

Because all six of us 5C actors had become friends, the telephone links between us now vibrated with our aggrieved calls, saying how LWT was shitting on us from a great height. I suppose we were all insecure as actors, wondering if it was a bluff about recasting if we insisted on them honouring the contracts. We probably thought that as our characters were not so firmly established with only seven episodes under our belts, and there being hundreds of other young hopefuls waiting for an opportunity to be cast in a television series, then LWT might pick on someone as an example and recast.

What we should have done, we all hypothesized years later, was to stick together and refuse to rescind the spring contract. It was doubtful they would have cast every single 5C character with entirely different actors. But doesn't hindsight create easy solutions?

I agreed to allow them to revoke the contract and accepted the new one starting much later in the year, as did all the others.

The year was off to a terrible start. Thinking the second series of *Please Sir!* was imminent, I turned down a small theatre job. And money from the first series would barely last until the end of February. It now became a huge struggle to live. I was fortunate that my loyal employers at Drury Lane Theatre, where I had worked off and on since my student days, gave me another stage-hand job, but this was part time, and just about covered our rent. I can recall one time of not having enough fare to catch the Tube at Archway to get to Leicester Square for the evening show at Drury Lane, so I had to set off early and walk at least two Tube stops. I walked as far as Kentish Town, from where I could afford the return fare, and as I walked I kept looking at the ground, hoping I might find some money and be able to get on at Tufnell Park, having only walked one stop.

No such luck. Where is that coin in the gutter when you need it?

The show at Drury Lane was the musical *Mame*, starring the legendary Ginger Rogers. I discovered her dresser was leaving, and they were looking for someone else to dress her. I told Zélie, she applied for the job, and was soon dressing Fred Astaire's famous dancing partner. Ginger Rogers was a Christian Scientist, only drank mineral water, and Zélie was often sent on errands to buy the star a bottle of her special spring water, not so readily available back then.

It is customary for actors to tip their dressers at the end of each week, and most actors, and even the chorus, gave their dressers at least a pound. Ginger Rogers tipped Zélie five shillings. But at least there were now two part-time salaries coming in. And there was another positive from working at Drury Lane in *Mame*. I met and became lifelong friends with Bob Bayne, a Glaswegian who later married and moved to Leeds, working as a prop buyer for Yorkshire Television. After we moved to a bigger flat in Highgate, Bob lodged with us for a while as we had two bedrooms, and he occasionally came to Wembley to see a recording of the show. We didn't see so much of each other once he moved to Leeds, although whenever I worked at the Leeds Grand Theatre, he always came to see a performance and we would have a drink afterwards.

A little bit of relief financially towards the end of February when I was interviewed by television director John Glenister, and the producer of *Thirty Minute Theatre*, Innes Lloyd. I was offered the part of Gunther Goettling, a young East German student. The play was called *Frontier*, written by Don

Shaw, based on a true incident when Peter Fechter, a young East German was shot trying to escape across the Berlin Wall. In *Frontier,* my character attempts an escape across a minefield and has his leg blown off, and while he lies in no-man's land slowly dying, neither the East nor West German military attempt to rescue him.

I was pleased to reacquaint myself with my old friend Larry Dann, with whom I attended Corona Academy Stage School in the late '50s and early '60s. We had already worked quite a few times together, and he was playing Lieutenant Klein, an East German border guard. Larry went on to have a successful career and had a long stint in *The Bill* as Sgt Peters.

Having rehearsed in the usual west London church hall for three days, on Thursday evening we were taken for a night shoot at a remote Army training ground, about an hour's drive from Television Centre. We the actors were ferried out to the location by mini-bus. When we got there, apart from the outside broadcast vans and unit vehicles, we saw that this no-man's land looked authentic with its thick forest trees and high barbed wire fence through which I would use my wire cutters to escape across the minefield until my leg was blown off. An observation tower manned by a sentry rose out of the ground in the gloom, and scenic designers had built temporary huts for the military, both East and West Germans, to discuss the problem of who should risk going into the minefield to rescue the student. The O.B. cameras were positioned in the distance, as if they were covering sporting events, almost hidden behind the trees. Most of the scenes would be performed without a break, and we could see which cameras were shooting by the red lights glowing in the dark. Strange how this drama based on a true event became so very real as the recording progressed. Suddenly we were hit by a blizzard and the snow came down heavily. I lay for hours on the freezing ground while things went wrong because of the extreme conditions. Light bulbs exploded from the cold, and a technician had to climb a twenty-five-foot ladder to replace them. The cameras froze, and Innes Lloyd, the producer, came out of the O.B. vehicle to help unfreeze them. Someone managed to get me a wetsuit, and I changed into it in the Portaloo. There were no portable dressing rooms of course, because the dressing rooms were back at Television Centre in White City where we had changed into our costumes. Despite the wetsuit I was still frozen, my teeth chattering and my body trembling with the cold. But the most discomfort I suffered was because I needed a crap, and there was no way I was going to undress again in the unheated Portaloo. I clenched

11

my buttocks tightly and ended up being constipated for the next three or four days.

Now, what should have been a night shoot ending before midnight, went on into the early hours of the morning. And because cameras were still freezing as the blizzard raged, and light bulbs popped melodically, the production dragged on, and I was told I would have to suffer the same torturous performance the following night.

Occasionally I was able to grab a hot drink and watch the other scenes, as Larry Dann as Lieutenant Klein discussed the problem of rescuing the student with Corporal Schabe, played by Tom Baker.

After the shoot, when taxis were summoned to take us home from Television Centre, they discovered Tom Baker lived in Archway, just a stone's throw from Highgate Village, and we shared the ride home. We chatted and became friends, and Tom often came up to the Village for a drink. While we waited for the pubs to open, we walked round Highgate Cemetery. Tom pointed out that opposite Karl Marx's tomb was the grave of a man named Spencer.

At first, I looked blank, until Tom grinned and said pointedly, 'Where do you buy your underwear?'

'Oh,' I said as the penny dropped. '*Marx* and Spencer!'

I later discovered the grave opposite Karl Marx was Herbert Spencer's, another political theorist, though Spencer's politics were, somewhat ironically, of the ideological liberal sort and polar opposite to that of his legendary neighbour.

When *Frontier* was transmitted and I watched it on television, I saw how effectively tense everyone was in the freezing temperature. No acting was required. This was reality.

Not long after this numbed performance, I auditioned and was offered the part of a male prostitute in the *W. Somerset Maugham* series, based on one of his short stories, *A Man with a Conscience*. The play starred Keith Barron as Jean Charvin, a man accused of murdering his wife and sent to Devil's Island, a brutal French penal colony, and was directed by a Frenchman, Henri Safran who always seemed to be absent from the rehearsal room when he took dozens of phone calls. John Glyn Jones, playing the second lead in the production, implied that because Safran was French he was probably on the phone to his mistress.

An action I found abhorrent was having to spit in Keith's face when Charvin rejects my advances. Keith told me to go for it once we were in the studio and not to hold back. Which I did, of course, and the reaction from his character was well-judged.

In make-up prior to the recording, a make-up woman tried to give an extra a greasy, sweaty look to his hair. 'You ain't slapping that shit on my hair,' he protested as she was about to slap a handful of grease onto his head. She pointed to me, dishevelled and dirtily disgusting, and told him how great I looked for a convict in a penal colony. 'It's all right for him,' answered the extra. 'He's an actor.'

During a lull in rehearsals, I can remember talking to Ruth Kettlewell, an ageing actress, who looked like everyone's quintessential maiden aunt. I told her about my gaff with a television director from years ago, when I was known by my birth name of Meurig Wyn-Jones and attended the first night of a West End play. In the interval I spotted an actor I thought I knew in the bar. I approached him and apologised for forgetting his name but said I could vaguely remember we worked together at some time. Looking miffed, the man said, 'Meurig, you won't get anywhere in this business if you can't remember a director's name, especially one you worked for only six weeks ago.'

When I told Ruth Kettlewell this story she apologised in advance for being able to top it, telling me that after attending an interview at the BBC she thought she would have lunch in the canteen and was surprised to see a face she knew. Just like me, she asked the chap where they had worked together. 'Darling,' the chap replied. 'I've just interviewed you!'

But unlike me and director David Boisseau, her director had a great sense of humour and she got the part. Later I remembered where I had worked for David Boisseau, although I have forgotten the name of the production. It was in a television play in Bristol, and the leading man was Kenneth Griffith. I had seen him in so many films and greatly admired his performances, especially with Peter Sellers and Mai Zetterling in the Kingsley Amis story set in Swansea, *Only Two Can Play,* with a screenplay by Bryan Forbes, in which Griffith played Ieuan Jenkins, a subservient character with a bad comb-over, a role in which he was extremely funny. He also played a major role in the cult horror film *Circus of Horrors* in 1960.

After the camera rehearsal in the Bristol TV studio, I was invited with the rest of the cast out to dinner. Griffith wouldn't let me pay and insisted on treating me. I may not have been able to recall much about the drama, but I can remember a story Griffith told us over dinner about working at Bristol Old Vic with Peter O'Toole, a year after Griffith's appearance in *Circus of Horrors* and a while before O'Toole became famous in *Lawrence of Arabia.*

They shared a flat in Clifton, and after a drinking session late one night, Kenneth Griffith left O'Toole to it, and went walking to get some air and to sober up. Unfortunately, there had been a murder in Clifton earlier that night, and he was apprehended by the police. He explained to them he could account for his whereabouts if they took him back to his flat, where his actor friend would vouch for him, and provide him with an alibi. But when police rang the flat doorbell, an inebriated O'Toole stuck his head out of an upstairs window and, recalling his friend's recent triumph in the horror film, pointed at him accusingly and yelled, 'That's him! The monster from hell. He's a monster! Well done for arresting him!'

During the studio recording of *A Man With a Conscience* at Television Centre, Verity Lambert took over the direction. Perhaps John Glyn Jones had been wrong about Safran. Maybe the director had to deal with something personal.

Although the second series of *Please Sir!* was not due to start rehearsing and recording until early September, John Alderton invited most of us to an Apollo 11 moon landing party on 20 July at his London flat, where we stayed up all night to see the memorable event. A friend of John's, Geoffrey Hughes, who was due to play a painter and decorator in the first episode of the second series of *Please Sir!*, attended the party and cooked us pancakes throughout the night. However shadowy the moonwalking astronaut figures of Armstrong and Aldrin were, we were all enthralled as we talked about the enormity of this technological achievement, and the distance that separated them from the earth. We all agreed it was a staggering achievement, although we did enjoy a few laughs that night as well, especially when President Richard Nixon came online to speak to the astronauts, saying it had to be the most historical phone call ever made, and Geoffrey Hughes wondered how much the call was costing, and if he had enough coins to feed in before the pips went. It was a great night though, and wonderful being part of this historic and memorable event, sharing it with our work colleagues, although I don't think Peter Cleall attended because he lived in Brighton, but I can certainly remember Peter Denyer and Malcolm McFee being there.

Prior to the moon landing, David Bowie's single 'Space Oddity' was released on 11 July and gave him his first No. 1 single when it was rereleased in 1975. Once he became a major rock star, in years to come, whenever I needed to contact a producer or director at a production company and gave the receptionist my name, I always heard breathless excitement in her voice and I was usually connected to my contact right away. But when it was discovered I was David Barry and not Bowie, I often detected a trace of disappointment in the director's voice.

Prior to the first episode *They're Off* being recorded, we spent half a day filming the opening titles where I give Bernard Hedges a V-sign and raspberry. We were all looking forward, not only to performing in the more conventional half-hour format, but also in colour. Years later, in the late eighties, I watched an episode of the quiz show *Telly Addicts*, and one of the questions asked was: 'What was the first ITV comedy to be broadcast in colour?' To my surprise the answer was *Please Sir!* I hadn't known that at the time, and I'm not even sure if it's true.

During this first episode, Geoffrey Hughes's painter and decorator, named Mr Turner (a subtlety which was lost on the studio audience), is still painting the classroom as 5C returns for their first day at school. What I had great admiration for in this episode was a speech of Peter Cleall's in which he rattles off a list of horses, remembering the odds on an accumulator bet, and how much each one wins when the next horse romps home. This got a big laugh when Hedges says, 'I thought you couldn't do fractions, Duffy.' And the reply came, 'They ain't fractions chief, they're odds.'

Peter Denyer was our Equity Deputy, and he discovered that for the opening titles film clip we were all entitled to an extra weekly fee, which Equity insisted on LWT paying. Mark Stuart went berserk, but he was stuck with it as far as this series was concerned. Mark often went berserk. I've never known a director with such a short fuse. He was calm in rehearsals, but the pressure of the studio got to him and if there was the slightest noise he would yell: 'You're on my time, Goddammit!'

Thankfully, rehearsals were a lot less traumatic. And if the mornings went well, which they invariably did, the lunchtimes became boozy affairs, playing silly games in the bar. One lunchtime, Mark, who was in his early fifties, accused John Esmonde, who was much younger than him, of being far less fit. A challenge reared its ridiculous head. A fiver was wagered on the writer attempting to beat the director, running from the ground floor to the bar on the twentieth floor, a punishing forty flights of stairs. They went down in the lift while we all waited. A little while later Mark strutted into the bar, breathing heavily but otherwise quite relaxed. John Esmonde stumbled in later, panting and pale-faced, barely able to speak. But he was too competitive to acknowledge defeat. He claimed age was on his side and challenged Mark to run the race again. Double or quits. But Mark was an ex-dancer and choreographer, a champion diver, regular squash player and trampolinist. He was genuinely fit. The only thing John had going for him was his competitive personality. When they ran the second race, we thought Bob Larbey would have to find another writing partner. Not only did John lose the race, he looked as if he was about to expire. He shook and couldn't speak for quite some time and had to be given another cognac transfusion.

Mark used to direct some of the Tommy Cooper shows. The comedian was at the bar one day and Mark brought him over and introduced us. The great accident-prone magician sat at our table and made a great big fuss of wanting to buy us all a drink. Unfortunately for us, and fortunately for him, he told us that he kept his money in a handkerchief, with at least half a dozen knots surrounding it. As he struggled to undo a single knot, not only did he make us laugh but he managed to get out of buying a round.

Mark had already told us the story of one of Cooper's favourite tricks. If a car was sent to pick him up, at the end of the journey the comedian would say to the driver, 'Thank you. Have a drink on me.' And he would shove what felt like a wad of notes into the driver's breast pocket. It turned out to be a tea bag.

As Tommy Cooper used his avaricious hankie trick on us, Mark was equally keen to get some good-humoured revenge. Cooper began telling us a long and elaborate joke. Mark whispered to someone in our group, 'Make an excuse and walk away. But first pass it on.' It took a while for the comedian to cotton on to what was happening, but by the time he neared the tagline of his gag he had lost his audience, and there was a look of desperation on his face as he belted out the punchline to the one person he physically restrained.

Playing practical jokes and winding people up happened regularly during rehearsals. LWT had small pads of notepaper with their logo at the top, and occasionally someone would get a message scribbled on one of these pads to call their agent during a break in rehearsals. We the naughty grown-up kids played a joke on Richard 'Dickie' Davies once. He got a message from his agent to ring such and such a number and speak to Mr Lyon or, if he wasn't there, to ask for Mr Fox. When Dickie made his call, he came back and told us how the conversation went.

'Hello. Could I speak to Mr Lyon?'

Pause. Then, 'Are you trying to be funny?'

'No, no. If he's not there I was told I could speak to Mr Fox.'

'This is Regent's Park Zoo.'

Another time, during a break in camera rehearsals at Wembley Studios, we were sitting in the canteen, when I brought out a page I had torn out of a copy of the Irish *Spotlight* when I was in Ireland. (*Spotlight* is a publication containing photographs of actors which casting directors can view when casting.) I handed my page round the canteen table. The photographs were three amateurish poses of an actor called Ben Bristow. The first photograph was captioned 'Drama' and was a picture of the Irish actor sporting a dreadful make-up, including an obviously false moustache, posing in fear as if a Hammer House of Horror ghoul was about to drag him to hell. Beneath the next picture it said 'Comedy' and showed Ben in an enormous plaid jacket, like an itinerant bookmaker, a finger pointing upwards, highlighting a brilliant punchline. The final picture was 'Variety', and the actor now had a ventriloquist's dummy sitting on his lap.

As the picture was passed around the table, everyone had a laugh at Ben's expense. Until it came to John Alderton. Stony-faced. Not the trace of a smile. 'What's funny about this?' he demanded.

I was taken aback. At first, I tried to explain what was funny but soon realised it was self-explanatory. Then John went on to say that Ben was an old friend of his and a fine actor. 'You're winding me up, John,' I protested. He threw the page onto the table and looked disgusted. I began to squirm. And others at the table began to shift uncomfortably and stared into their coffee cups. Then John went too far, telling me that Ben's wife had just died of cancer, how much he missed her and was finding it hard to cope. Now I knew I was being sent up.

We also found a great way to entertain everyone in the studio canteen. If any of the studio floor managers needed someone paged to the studio, they used an internal phone, usually situated between two heavy doors leading to the studio. We began to put in some false calls. Sitting in the canteen, people often heard announcements along the lines of: 'Could Mr Albert Bridge go to Studio Three in five minutes, please?'

None of the telephonists seemed to twig. We got away with all kinds of names, everyone from Joe Stalin to Bill Shakespeare or Jane Austen. Then one day I picked up the internal phone and put in a call for Miss Connie Lingus to go to Studio Three. 'Who's that?' the telephonist demanded. 'This isn't a proper call, is it?'

Clearly there was nothing wrong with the telephonist's sex education.

One lunchtime we were on the studio floor, surrounded by all the mess and tangle of camera cables. Apart from us 'kids' and John Alderton, the studio was empty, everyone having gone to lunch. John suddenly folded his arms and began hopping on one leg. It was a game we all knew, where you hop about, barge against someone and try to knock them off balance. The loser is the one who must use both legs or risk being pushed over. We had only just started the game when John tripped on one of the camera cables and sprained his ankle. While we helped him out of the studio we agreed to keep quiet about the ridiculous game. As he limped badly, we helped him to where Mark sat in the canteen. At first, Mark looked worried, wondering how his leading actor was going to get through the night's recording. After John had visited the studio nurse, got his ankle bound up, and limped back into the canteen, he told Mark he couldn't possibly drive to Weybridge and the studio must provide a car to take him home after the recording. Mark then went into cynical overdrive and point blank refused to increase his budget for a car, telling John he would have to pay for his own taxi. John protested that it was a studio accident, tripping over the camera cables. But Mark then said something along the lines of: '*I* know you were mucking about, John. *You* know you were mucking about. And *you* know *I* know you were mucking about.'

After the recording, which John managed to get through without much obvious limping, we all headed for the bar. By now, Mark and John were in deep sulks and not talking to one another.

When we began rehearsals for the next episode, Peter Cleall and I watched as John stood awkwardly next to Mark at the coffee point. Then one of them made a move, offering to pour coffee for the other, which was accepted gracefully. The quarrel was over. As we observed this touching, cinematic scene, Peter and I giggled as we imagined how it would look in slow motion and soft focus.

Mark was an active man, and once he'd completed his camera script by the morning of day three, everyone relaxed, and most of us younger cast members would disappear into an adjacent and empty rehearsal room to play handball on a court Mark had mapped out with gaffer tape. He provided gloves and tennis balls, explained the rules to us, then enjoyed beating us. God knows what guest actors coming in to do one episode thought as the producer/director disappeared to play games with some of his actors.

We also played cricket with balls made from compressed newspaper covered in gaffer tape. These elliptical missiles were quite hard, and John bowled as if it was county cricket he was playing. Strip fluorescent lights got smashed, crashing spectacularly to the floor, then the shards had to be swept up and concealed behind cupboards. Strangely, nobody from LWT ever mentioned this damage.

Erik Chitty occasionally behaved just like his Smithy character. When we were about halfway through the series, he approached Peter and me, and asked why Eric Duffy was called El. We explained that East Londoners often do that – calling someone by the name of Derek 'Del' or Terry 'Tel', which was why the script often referred to Eric as 'El'. There was a pause before Erik Chitty said, 'Oh, I see. But no one has ever called me El.'

It gave us the giggles, and we later referred to him as El Chitty

The series was phenomenally successful, and every episode reached the top ten in the viewing figures. Frank Muir had been replaced by Barry Took as Head of Entertainment, and he was wonderfully friendly and supportive.

Peter Cleall, who was an active Labour supporter and party member, had been campaigning for them, and was convinced it may have been the reason he was refused a bank loan. As soon as he had a copy of the signed contract for the second series, he approached his bank manager for a loan to put down as a deposit for a flat. The bank manager flatly refused, telling Peter he couldn't give a loan on money that hadn't yet been earned. Peter rightly pointed out that it was a solid contract, couldn't be broken, and the substantial amount of money would come in weekly for thirteen weeks. Apart from which, if he already earned the money, he wouldn't need a loan. But the bank manager stubbornly refused, and it occurred to Peter that he may have been seen in his district by the bank manager, campaigning for the Labour Party, and that was the reason for the loan refusal. During a lunch break during the first rehearsal, Peter happened to tell Barry Took this story about the intransigent bank manager. Took then kindly offered to get Peter an advance from Artistes' Payments, which could be deducted from his television fee each week. And he didn't go back on his word. Peter got his loan from LWT instead of the bank.

Whenever we did exterior filming, the series was so popular with young people, we were invariably mobbed as they clamoured for autographs. When we finished rehearsals, which always coincided with the time secondary schoolchildren went home, we tried to keep a low profile, hiding behind sunglasses and broadsheet newspapers. On our own we were less of a target. Collectively there was more of a danger of being recognised.

Once, on our journey to Euston from Stonebridge Park, in one of those single compartment carriages, Peter Denyer got off at Queens Park to cross to the other side of the platform to catch a Tube train. The platform swarmed with teenagers, and Peter kept a low profile, head buried in his newspaper.

He went unnoticed as he stood in the heart of the throng. Until our train began to pull out. Peter Cleall, Liz and I lowered the carriage window, pointed excitedly at the poor sod and yelled, 'Look! That bloke in sunglasses. That's Dennis Dunstable.' The teenagers descended on the unfortunate actor like a plague of locusts.

Although working in *Please Sir!* sounds as if it was all just fun and games, it had its downside. Occasionally we became nervous, gibbering wrecks, and it was all down to Mark Stuart who used to rule his actors like a demented cattle-trail boss. Rehearsals were not so bad, it was when we got into the studio that the fireworks would start. Whenever he shouted at the slightest noise, the veins stood out on his neck and people feared for their lives. I was doing a scene with John Alderton in an episode, and Mark asked me to pause for a quick reaction shot from John. During the camera run-through I forgot. The floor manager told me to hold it. And then I heard the control room door being flung open and feet pounding along the catwalk above the studio. And then a let-there-be-light voice blazed across the studio, 'Barry! What about that pause?'

During the camera rehearsal of a boxing scene in *The Sporting Life*, Mark came pounding down onto the studio floor, stormed up to an extra and screamed at him, 'Your lifeless, boring face is in the back of my shot. For Christ's sake react. Do something.' The extra turned to jelly. Unconcerned, Mark turned away and delivered his next line to the studio. 'Wood. Fucking wood.'

Mark knew how to play to the gallery. Always. But he didn't fool many with his temper tantrums. Like the camp vision mixer who, having listened to one of his tirades, threw out an aside. 'I missed his last Western.' Or the world-weary prop man behind the scenes, who muttered following one of Mark's slavering outbursts, 'I've seen cunts come, and I've seen cunts go, but that cunt's the biggest actor of them all.'

As far as the studio staff and technicians were concerned, these outbursts were interesting incidents to break up the rehearsal. But for us, the younger actors, it was nerve-wracking. We knew Mark hated to do much editing, which was time and money, so he instilled so much fear into us so that when we performed the shows in front of the studio audience, we didn't dare stumble, fluff or dry. Our shows were complete theatre performances with no retakes. Retakes were *verboten*. If there were any mistakes, these were broadcast, so that millions of viewers witnessed our gaffs. Consequently, we rarely made mistakes.

In fairness to Mark, his tyrannical behaviour vanished after the recordings, and he often pushed the boat out in the bar to make amends. He was never a person to hold a grudge.

Mark lived close to me in Highgate Village, around the corner on North Hill. He asked me to call round on several occasions, saying we might pop into the Gatehouse pub. I called at his house one day and found him watching *Peyton Place* with the sound turned off. When I asked him about this, he said he liked to guess the shot sequences and call them up in advance, and said he was often right.

Usually the outside filming sequences were shot on what would have been the second day of rehearsal. Episode four, *The Sporting Life*, the swimming pool scenes were shot at the large Olympic-size pool at Crystal Palace. The tag to the first half was Dennis Dunstable losing his oversize swimming trucks as he climbs out of the water. Peter Denyer was terribly nervous about doing this scene, especially as one of the wardrobe men had to assist on covering his genitals with plaster, as the shot was of his naked buttocks from the back. And however nervous he was about his naked appearance, we didn't help matters by reminding him every few minutes, which was another of our wind ups.

There was more outside filming for the next episode, *Norman's Conquest*, with a trip to London zoo. This was what they called 'wild filming', most of it unscripted and we could make it up as we went along. As we walked past an enclosure containing an intense-looking coypu, someone suggested it looked like Erik Chitty as Smithy. Mark got the cameraman to film it, then when we were in Wembley Studio for this episode, prior to the dress rehearsal, Mark asked Erik Chitty if he would sit in one of the chairs in the staffroom and stare thoughtfully at the camera. He wanted to know why, and Mark told him it was an insert in case they needed it. But when the film sequence was shown, with Erik's face superimposed onto the coypu's, he took it as an insult and became upset.

We all felt a bit guilty after this childish prank; it was nothing personal but Erik didn't see it that way. In any case, our producer and director was as much to blame as us overgrown kiddies.

After the recordings most of us would go out for a Chinese or Indian meal, which eventually became another bone of contention between Mark and John. As the leading actor in the series, John used to warm-up the studio audience, thus saving payment to a warm-up man. John one day sprang it on Mark that LWT ought to cough up for our meal as payment for him doing the warm-up. Mark refused. John continued to do the warm-up but told Mark that if there was a third series he wouldn't do it.

As I write and record this, it is 2020, and one of the mighty Hollywood producers has tumbled from his powerful perch. I mean of course Harvey Weinstein. I mention this because it reminded me of an incident Malcolm McFee told us about. He wanted a part in *Virgin Soldiers* which was to be filmed in Malaya by theatre director John Dexter. Malcolm's agent arranged for him to meet the director who took him to dinner at the Ivy. Following dinner, Dexter took Malcolm back to his flat for a nightcap. Malcolm, still thinking he could handle the situation, and thinking he might still be in with a chance for a part in this major film, gently pointed out that he liked John Dexter but that he wasn't himself gay. 'That's all right,' the director said. 'We'll just wank.' Which was when Malcolm made an excuse and left. The next day Malcolm got a call from his agent who told him that John Dexter had telephoned in a rage, saying, 'Who the fuck does Malcolm McFee think he is? If he thinks there's a part for him in *Virgin Soldiers* he can go and fuck himself.'

Malcolm, when he told us this story, did admit that perhaps he had been naïve. But he was only eighteen-years-old when it happened, so his naivety is perfectly understandable. The blame lies with all the Weinstein-like shits who use and abuse their power for sex. Now, had John Dexter not held a grudge because of Malcolm's rejection of his advances, and still cast him in his film, he might have been less despicable.

For each episode of the series we had the same group of non-speaking young actors in our 5C class. They didn't attend rehearsals but arrived at Wembley Studio for the camera rehearsals. One of the weekly regulars was George Georghio, who was of Greek origin, and they cast him as a young Asian lad in the third episode, *Panalal Passes By*, which he played excellently. It was in this episode we were first introduced to a 5C parent, my mother Mrs Abbott, played by Barbara Mitchell in a short café scene in which she and Abbott join Hedges at his table and she puts him off his food by talking about her operation. It was the first time she called me her 'little soldier'. Barbara was perfect casting for my mother and extremely funny, and I just knew we would see a great deal more of her in future episodes.

The second time we were introduced to one of 5C's parents was in episode seven, *The Decent Thing*, in which Bernard Hedges after a boozy night wakes up in Sharon's mother's bedroom and can't remember the night before. Diana Coupland played Connie Eversleigh. Born in Leeds in 1928, Coupland became a professional singer aged 14, and sang in ballrooms and hotels like the Dorchester and Savoy throughout the '50s and '60s. Two years after her performance in *Please Sir!* she was introduced to another Abbott when she became Sidney James's wife in *Bless This House,* the sitcom about the Abbott family which ran until Sidney James's death in 1976.

They say religious converts are the most devout, and this was certainly true of Deryck Guyler, a Catholic convert. When we rehearsed our classroom scenes, he often sat in a corner of the rehearsal room reading his Bible. But Deryck was a lovely bloke, and never proselytised or even mentioned religion, keeping it to himself. He did, however, have one bête noire, and this was the actress Rita Webb. Her language was so crudely profane that he feared for his sensibilities. Consequently, we often wound Deryck up by pretending we had already glimpsed next week's script and Rita Webb was joining us as guest performer. Deryck blanched at the thought but laughed along with it when he realized we were pulling his leg. In fact, more than anyone else, Deryck was the one who corpsed hugely during the recording of one episode, when the actress playing the school cook in the scene opposite him said something and ejaculated her false teeth. Deryck laughed uncontrollably and it took him quite a while to get back into character, even after the actress tucked her teeth back in and restarted the scene.

With great dialogue and storylines from Esmonde and Larbey, the second series became hugely successful – and I think a contributing factor may have been because we all got on so well. There was never any division between the staff members and us so-called school kids. At lunchtime, we all spent time together in the London Weekend bar. Even the dragon of Fenn Street School, 'Miss Doris Rotten Ewell' as played by Joan Sanderson, I can remember was far removed from her character. She once spilt white wine over me in the London Weekend bar, and just giggled apologetically because it had gone to her head.

Joan was married to Gregory Scott, an actor who came into the studio each week to play a non-speaking teacher. He was a nice chap, but I often used to wonder how he must have felt working as an extra while his wife played one of the leading roles.

Every single episode of the second series was in the top twenty ratings, reaching a high of Number 3 with *The Generation Gap*, in which Peter Craven takes responsibility in assisting a recalcitrant and lonely pensioner played by Jack Woolgar. We guessed we would meet again for a third series in 1970, although we were starting to look a little long in the tooth to be sitting behind desks, which detractors mentioned at every opportunity. But part of the success of the series was the way John and Bob had written it so that we in 5C were far more street-wise than Bernard Hedges, the rather naïve but dedicated teacher.

5C and Dylan Thomas

The following year, with my character well-established on television, I was offered a summer season at Torquay in *Don't Tell the Wife,* a farcical comedy by Sam Cree, which would star Jack Douglas as Alf the plumber and I was to play Cyril, the plumber's mate. Although Jack was very professional and quite funny, we never really hit it off. During rehearsals, he would ask me to put in lines about various brands of whisky or beer and was quite cagey about explaining the reasons for this when I asked him. Then it transpired, during the run at Torquay, all kinds of freebie booze would be delivered to his dressing room, none of which he ever shared.

It was 1970, and after more than six years of a Labour government, Prime Minister Harold Wilson was about to be ousted in the forthcoming election. Jack Douglas, was a fervent Tory and, following the shows, he made a curtain speech extolling the virtues of Edward Heath and the Conservatives. Being a Labour supporter, I objected to having to stand on stage during the curtain call as if I also gave my support to the Tories. Joan Mann, an actress who came from the South Wales valleys, also objected to his political curtain speeches, and we both went to his dressing room and complained, suggesting we might stand down from the curtain call if he continued to make a political speech. We pointed out that whatever a person's political persuasion, putting a political message across following a show was just not on. It didn't go down well with Jack.

Another time, he was invited to a police event, a buffet and cabaret, and as my character from *Please, Sir!* was popular, I was invited as well. But when Zélie and I watched a comedian, and heard racist jokes along the lines of, 'There was this Paki running a bed and breakfast, and he answers the door to a guest while carrying a pitchfork, saying he was just about to make up the beds', we decided it was time to leave. The police in the climate of the day thought this sort of material was hilarious.

Our walking out of this event early didn't go unnoticed by Jack Douglas, who clearly liked to keep in with people he thought mattered, and it was probably another bad mark against me. Which worked to my advantage because London Weekend Television got in touch with my agent about doing a third series of *Please, Sir!* Because Jack Douglas's brother was one of the producers of the Torquay show, and from what Jack had probably told him about me, they were only too glad to see the back of me and agreed to let me go before the season ended. Fortunately, Max Bygraves's son Anthony happened to live in Torquay, and he took over my part.

While working in Torquay, I bought my first car, a sit-up-and-beg vehicle, a tiny Austin A40. And, having been released from the Jack Douglas season, it was Zélie who drove us back to London as I still needed a few lessons from a professional driving instructor before applying for my test. We broke down halfway back to London, and we spent well over an hour getting a repair done at a garage, while we worried about our cat, Parsley, stuck in his basket on this sweltering hot day. We had inherited Parsley from Peter Denyer, whose Siamese cat had had kittens. Parsley was a lovely creature, but unfortunately he went missing when we were back in Highgate and we never discovered what happened to him.

It was during this year I attended a casting interview for the Granada Television comedy *The Lovers,* starring Richard Beckinsale and Paula Wilcox. I was interviewed by writer Jack Rosenthal and director Michael Apted. When I was asked about what recent work I had done, I naturally mentioned *Please Sir!* Rosenthal and Apted turned to each other and had a long discussion, almost as if I was not in the room, about how much they disliked the series, and how all the characters were stereotypes, especially Deryck Guyler's character. Their behaviour was rude and unsettling, and I should have said something. But I didn't. I only thought of what I should have done when I came away from the interview, wishing I had a rewind button.

Sam Fonteyn's distinctive theme tune remained the same for the third series of *Please Sir!* But Mark Stuart made certain the opening titles didn't use any actors other than John Alderton. He was probably still smarting from having to budget for the extra payments for the second series. Now we had the much cheaper credits scrawled like graffiti on brick walls.

One of the pleasures of working in the series was in getting a new script and reading some of John and Bob's stage directions. I can remember how funny some of them were, like the one where Doris Ewell is being driven by the headmaster, who changes gear and inadvertently touches her knee. The stage direction read, 'Miss Ewell's cup runneth over.'

The first episode of the new series, *Ag Bow Rumber*, had Bob Todd playing another character, a neurotic man in charge of the boats by a lake in the park, a filmed scene with Penny Spencer and John Alderton, in which Todd ends up in the lake. Bob did this stunt himself, probably while fortified by a few large vodkas as his daily alcohol consumption was epic. Also appearing in the first episode was Barrie Gosney as Clarkie, a scrap metal dealer who gives Dunstable a job. Barrie Gosney went on to star in *Time Gentlemen Please* and the *Harry Hill* comedy shows. And this was the episode in which we are introduced to Hedges' girlfriend Penny Wheeler, played by Jill Kerman, although most of us actors wouldn't meet her until episode two, as her first appearance was on film with John.

Prior to this series starting, John Alderton had played Malcolm in *Macbeth* on BBC Television. Malcolm McFee showed me a review he'd seen in the *Daily Telegraph*, which said something like 'John Alderton's lop-shouldered Malcolm is similar to his Bernard Hedges character, so much so that one expects to see Abbott and Craven coming through Burnum Wood.' Daringly, Malcolm said to John, 'I see David and I got a review in your *Macbeth*, John, and we weren't even in it.'

John stared frostily at Malcolm as icicles formed on the rehearsal room ceiling. I never knew with John, who was a master of inscrutability, whether it was double bluff and he was just turning the wind up around.

Episode Two featured Barbara Mitchell's second appearance as my mother when Frankie ends up in hospital for an appendectomy. Barbara was great fun and a lovely person, and we all thought her characterisation of Mrs Abbott was brilliant and guessed she would be returning at some stage to appear in more episodes, although she didn't appear in any more of the third series, which concentrated more on our preparing to leave school, and Bernard's plans to marry his fiancée Penny Wheeler.

There must have been times at Wembley Studios when we had to hang around, and I really cannot remember why this was; but I can remember that during those times the six of us would go Tenpin Bowling, which was within walking distance of the studio.

During rehearsals for this third series, Richard Davies, who lived in Forest Hill with his wife Jill Britton (who was also an actor) and their two children, told us he had been approached by the manager of Lewisham Concert Hall who said he would love to have the cast of *Please Sir!* performing at his theatre and was confident he could fill this thousand seat venue.

Under Milk Wood was Richard's favourite play, and it was one we all loved, and so it was decided Peter Denyer would co-direct it with Richard. There were no problems with casting and we all fitted into the multitude of roles with no arguments. Richard's wife Jill joined the cast, as did my wife Zélie, and a friend of Dickie and Jill's, Joy Cox. As the production was for one night only, it was unreasonable to expect anyone to learn the Narrator, and a Welsh actor friend of Richard's, David Garfield, agreed to read the marathon part. When we finished rehearsing our latest *Please Sir!* episode, we loitered in the rehearsal room until everyone went home. A little later, Jill, Zélie and Joy Cox would arrive, our having told reception to expect them (things were a great deal more relaxed about security then). We rehearsed *Milk Wood* for two or three hours until the early evening, when it was time to adjourn to the LWT bar.

No one at LWT discovered we used their rehearsal room free of charge to rehearse our own play. But we reckoned that after the cancellation of the contracts in the spring of 1969, they owed us that much at least.

Because we were performing for one night only at Lewisham, we had to stage it as simply as possible. Someone had the idea of having us all sitting in a row beneath a long white sheet covering our heads, then when it was time for the Narrator to introduce each character's dreams, out would pop the actor's head.

Lewisham Concert Hall was an enormous venue, and as we waited under the sheet we couldn't hear any noise from the auditorium. Perhaps it was a washout, and nobody had turned up. But what we didn't realize was that the safety curtain was down. As soon as they started to raise it, the roar of the crowd overwhelmed us, and we began to feel seriously nervous. It was a full house. And Lewisham had advertised it in the *Evening Standard* London Theatre Guide, billing us as stars from *Please Sir!* in *Under Milk Wood,* with Duffy, Sharon, Abbott, Maureen, Dunstable, Craven and Mr Price, instead of our own names. I have no idea how Joan Sanderson came to be billed on the flyers as she had never agreed to be in the production, and I guess it may well have been an error on the part of Lewisham Concert Hall Management.

Penny Spencer played Mae Rose Cottage, Mrs Pugh and Mrs Dai Bread Two. There were no radio microphones that we could use, and Penny often had difficulty being heard when she played Sharon in the studio, when the boom operator came in as close as he dared without throwing shadows across actors' faces. We knew that being able to hear Penny in the vast Lewisham venue was going to be a problem, but Peter Denyer came up with a solution.

He had an actress friend who concealed herself behind the masking curtain behind Penny. As Penny delivered her lines, Peter's friend said them in unison so that the audience could hear them. This double-tracking effect, for all I know, was probably the first time anyone has been dubbed in live theatre.

Although the production may have been a bit short on production values, the play was an outstanding success that night. If the production lacked polish, what did it matter? The atmosphere and our enthusiasm, coupled with the anticipation and excitement of the audience, gave us the feeling that here was something unique, a happening or an event that could never be repeated.

Following the performance the manager came backstage and congratulated us, no doubt pleased with his box office takings for that night. As we took our time leaving the theatre the crowds who usually clamoured for autographs had mostly dispersed, although there were at least a dozen hearty autograph collectors waiting outside the stage door.

Liz was married to Ian Talbot, who eventually became artistic director at Regent's Park Open Air Theatre. Zélie and I became close friends with them, and on several occasions we went with them to their holiday cottage in Llanberis, where Liz's maternal grandmother lived. One evening, during the run of our series, we were round at Liz and Ian's flat in Kentish Town and Liz's mother, who lived upstairs, told us to switch on *News at Ten*. One of the news items showed their holiday cottage being occupied by Plaid Cymru or the Free Wales Army (I can't remember which dissident group it was), protesting about strangers buying properties for holiday use only. They probably picked

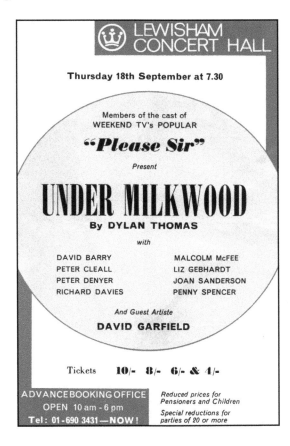

LEWISHAM CONCERT HALL

Thursday 18th September at 7.30

Members of the cast of WEEKEND TV's POPULAR

"*Please Sir*"

Present

UNDER MILKWOOD

By DYLAN THOMAS

with

DAVID BARRY
PETER CLEALL
PETER DENYER
RICHARD DAVIES

MALCOLM McFEE
LIZ GEBHARDT
JOAN SANDERSON
PENNY SPENCER

And Guest Artiste

DAVID GARFIELD

Tickets 10/- 8/- 6/- & 4/-

ADVANCE BOOKING OFFICE
OPEN 10 am - 6 pm
Tel: 01-690 3431 — NOW!

Reduced prices for Pensioners and Children
Special reductions for parties of 20 or more

Liz and Ian's cottage because she was an actress, her surname was Gebhardt (her father Joe was American) and thought it might be positive publicity for their cause. But what they hadn't realized when they broke a back window to gain access to the cottage was that Liz's mother was Welsh, and there was a solid local connection to the village. When Liz's grandmother called at the cottage and gave the dissidents a piece of her mind in the Welsh language, the rebels abandoned the cottage, having first left a cheque to pay for the broken window.

Many of the *Please Sir!* episodes were now directed by Alan Wallis, a vision mixer turned director. We all got along well with Alan, who was quiet, polite and competent, a complete contrast to Mark. But as Producer, Mark was still very much the boss, and liked us to know it. John Alderton, who during series two had bounced off our sometimes-improvised classroom behaviour, began to object, telling us to only do what was rehearsed and scripted. And he didn't seem to like Alan Wallis's direction. I had a scene with Liz in the empty classroom, and instead of politely suggesting a way to improve the scene, John stepped in, stood in front of the director, and proceeded to direct us himself. Alan didn't say anything. He was always very calm and laid-back. As soon as John finished giving us notes on how to play the scene, Alan stepped forward, lowered his voice, and told us to continue doing it in the way we had been playing it. John overheard this, and his face darkened.

Rehearsals were often interrupted by the media wanting interviews or photographs. When they wanted a photo of the 5C kids, the six of us would pose, and then a photographer would ask five of us to clear because he might want a solo shot of Penny in her mini-skirt, and we could all guess which photo would be used. When this happened, I used to feel sorry for Liz, but those press photographers can be very thick-skinned. But Liz always put a brave face on it and I never heard her complain.

In November we were taken to the bar at LWT by *Daily Mirror* reporter Ken Irwin. He bought John Alderton and us six 'kids' drinks, offered us cigars or cigarettes, then had his photographer take shots of us leaning against the bar, smoking and drinking. When he interviewed us, he asked mainly about our smoking and drinking habits. Lambs to the slaughter. We were playing schoolchildren, and what came out in the paper was that Frankie Abbott smokes three or four cigars a day and drinks Scotch, Eric Duffy drinks beer or white wine, Sharon Eversleigh drinks shandies but smokes twenty-five a day when she's working, Maureen Bullock drinks Scotch and smokes French cigarettes, Dennis Dunstable drinks Scotch or lager and smokes twenty a day

– plus, and Peter Craven 'smokes like a chimney' and 'drinks like a fish' – beer or vodka and tonic. By contrast, 'Sir', did none of these things and enjoyed Shakespeare, playing classical records, and was a dab hand at golf and cricket.

This is how reporters tried to tarnish the image of us little kiddies. Not that it bothered us. In fact it probably added more kudos to the fictional worldly 5C kids versus a naïve, liberal teacher and gave the show a boost. Anyway, who really remembers trivia from yesterday's paper?

And from NCRV, a Dutch television station in the Netherlands, a film camera crew might suddenly descend on the rehearsal room, and we would send filmed messages over to Holland. The series was hugely popular over there and a Dutch publisher had commissioned a couple of *Please Sir!* novelisations of two of the series. It was so popular in the Netherlands that when Zelie and I went to Amsterdam for a week's break, whenever we dined at a restaurant, often other customers would send us over drinks, then raise their glasses, saying 'Cheers, Mr Abbott!'

We also became a cartoon strip in the *Look-In* magazine, a junior version of the *TV Times* a periodical which became very popular with younger viewers.

Something I disliked about many episodes was the lack of sound in some of the filmed sequences. Because there was no written dialogue, everyone seemed to over-compensate by over-acting, and our performances were accompanied by rather twee find-us-funny music. I don't think there could have been technical reasons for this because there was scripted sound for the swimming scene in *The Sporting Life*.

Unlike the golf sequence shot at Mill Hill Golf Club for *The Honour of the School*, which again had that awful music covering acting without dialogue. Mind you, the day spent filming at the golf club was good fun, as we were able to play snooker in their billiard room in between takes. This episode featured Terence Alexander, who challenges Hedges to a game of golf for a hefty bet.

Terry Alexander was an affable, easy-going man, a familiar face on television, who had recently played Lord Uxbridge in the epic Sergei Bondarchuk film *Waterloo*, which starred Rod Steiger as Napoleon and Christopher Plummer as Wellington. But Terry is probably best remembered as the loveable rogue Charlie Hungerford in *Bergerac,* in which he appeared in 85 episodes.

The Honour of The School was the episode where Duffy loses his temper and grabs hold of Peter Craven, saying, 'You wanna watch yourself, Peter.' To

which Malcolm replied during the recording, 'Go on, hit me then, Peter.' The mistake either went unnoticed, or Mark Stuart left it in to ensure we always got everything a hundred per cent right with no chance of a retake. Perhaps he thought one transmission, with maybe one repeat, the mistakes would be forgotten, trusting in the belief that television episodes were ephemeral. He hadn't reckoned on the enormous video market which took off in the eighties, or DVDs in the late nineties, and so Malcolm's indelible gaff endures.

By now the series was incredibly popular, and it reached number one in the ratings for the episode *The Facts of Life* when it was broadcast in November, even beating *Coronation Street, Dad's Army* and *Steptoe and Son,* which meant more celebratory champagne in the bar at lunchtimes. We enjoyed meeting all the other sitcom casts as well, the *On The Buses* team and *Doctor in The House.* We got to know Anna Karen very well as her husband Terry Duggan played the barman in The Feathers, our Fenn Street pub.

Mark occasionally surprised us by his supportive actions. Like the time at the Wembley Studio self-service canteen when we arrived at the cashier's till with our food to be told there would be a two-shilling surcharge on all meals for freelance employees as opposed to LWT's permanent staff. We objected to this because we felt actors might earn good wages but only for a limited

TELEVISION'S TOP TWENTY

Position	Programme	Areas screened	Viewing homes (millions)
1	Please Sir! (London Weekend)	All	7.75
2	Steptoe and Son (BBC)	All	7.60
3	Coronation Street (Wednesday, November 4) (Granada)	All	7.55
4	Coronation Street (Monday, November 2) (Granada)	All	7.30
5	Opportunity Knocks! (Thames)	All	7.00
6	Armchair Theatre (The Dolly Scene) (Thames)	All	6.85
6	Dad's Army (BBC)	All	6.85
8	The Main Chance (Yorkshire)	All	6.70
9	Queenie's Castle (Yorkshire)	All	6.65
9	Fraud Squad (ATV)	All	6.65
11	News At Ten (Tuesday, November 3) (ITN)	All	6.50
12	Special Branch (Thames)	All	6.35
13	Softly, Softly (BBC)	All	6.30
14	World In Action (Granada)	All	6.25
14	The Lovers (Granada)	All	6.25
16	Blue Murder At St. Trinians (BBC)	All	6.20
17	News At Ten (Thursday, November 5) (ITN)	All	6.15
18	Mary Hopkin In The Land of Films (BBC)	All expect CS, NS	6.10
18	Boy On A Dolphin (BBC)	All	6.10
20	Z Cars (Tuesday, November 3) (BBC)	All	6.05

Chart compiled from JICTAR ratings for week ended November 8, 1970 time, whereas technicians were employed 52 weeks a year with paid holidays and sick leave. As our Equity Deputy, Peter Denyer approached the NATKE (National Association of Theatre and Kine Employees) shop steward to request support. But he was met with a cold shoulder. The NATKE shop steward shrugged it off, saying something like, 'Well, actors earn enough money.' Incensed, we refused to eat in the canteen, told Mark the predicament, and said we intended leaving the studio each lunchtime to get some food in Wembley. Mark, maybe scared of us getting back late from lunch, offered to send out for takeaways which he paid for. As soon as the catering manager saw what was happening, it wasn't long before the surcharge was removed.

Someone who clearly disapproved of the way we behaved as characters, and our sometimes risqué dialogue (mild by today's standards) was Mary Whitehouse of the National Viewers' and Listeners' Association. LWT often got complaints from her organisation, which we all thought was strange. Because our programme was broadcast at 7.25 p.m., before the nine o'clock watershed, it was a rule that each weekly script had to be sent to ITA (Independent Television Authority) to monitor their suitability for transmission during the early evening. It transpired that Mark's P.A. had been posting the scripts to the wrong address, and they lay abandoned on the floor of a vacant office building in Knightsbridge, along with piles of junk mail.

This couldn't have happened with the first series, as two out of the seven episodes were moved from their earlier transmission of 8.30 to a 9.15 slot, so I guess ITA must have insisted on this having read the scripts.

The last three episodes of the third series were broadcast in black and white because of a colour technicians' strike. The first of these episodes was *Situations Vacant*, and we were introduced to Mr Dunstable, Dennis's ghastly, drunken father. The part was played by eccentric actor Peter Bayliss, who arrived at rehearsals looking dapper, wearing a collar and tie and blue serge suit. He threw

> *Mr & Mrs Wheeler*
> *request the pleasure of your company*
> *at the wedding of their daughter*
>
> *PENELOPE to BERNARD HEDGES*
>
> *at St Mark's Church*
> *on Saturday 26th December 1970*
>
> *RSVP*

himself into the role, and you often wondered what strange exclamations would spring from his larynx, groans and grunts from deep down in his chest, and uncoordinated arm movements. His character took over, and the dapper actor went home at the end of rehearsals looking like a tramp.

I don't think John Alderton appreciated his way of performing. By now John wanted everything performed as was rehearsed, even to the slightest movement, expression or exclamation. During the recording of a scene with Peter Bayliss he suddenly stopped, and the floor manager stepped forward and asked what was wrong. John glared at Peter Bayliss and mentioned that he was thrown by a prop being placed in a different position. For a moment there was an uncomfortable atmosphere, and we imagined Mark seething up in the control room. The scene resumed, and the studio audience appeared not to notice the undercurrents of the performers.

Our final episode was a Christmas special, *And Everyone Came Too*, about Bernard and Penny's wedding to which we were all invited. It could have been a colourful ending, but the strike was still on and it was recorded and transmitted in black and white, which was disappointing. It would have been good to finish with the eye-catching colourful fashions at the end of the swinging sixties and the beginning of the early seventies.

The series became so popular it was sold to more than 40 countries and was enormously popular in Australia and New Zealand. And still reception at Wembley Studio didn't display any photographs from the show, even though they had pictures of *On the Buses, Doctor in The House, Within These Walls, The Gentle Touch* and many others.

To this day I have no idea why they chose to snub us in this way.

Pinewood Studios

We are in the Number One dressing room at the London Palladium waiting to be called onstage for the BAFTA Awards. We are here because John Alderton has been nominated for Best Actor for his performance as Bernard Hedges and Mark Stuart for Best Light Entertainment programme – namely *Please Sir!*. Esmonde and Larbey have written us a sketch – two lines each. The awards will be presented by David Frost. We had one brief rehearsal, without the presenter himself, and now we wait, hearts pounding. The reason we are all so nervous is because we will perform in front of a massive audience of famous actors, producers and directors. The two lines in my head keep vanishing. I'm panicking, because I can't refer to a script. A mere two lines, I remember thinking, why would I need a script for two lines? And now, as it gets closer to our appearance, and we hear applause on the show relay system, those two bloody lines keep disappearing from my brain. They do that tantalizingly, one minute here, the next moment gone.

John Alderton wears a dinner jacket and black bow tie, but we are dressed in our character costumes, me in my leather jacket and Penny in short skirt and high heels. She has removed her shoes for comfort. Big mistake, because the stage manager puts his head round the dressing room door, panic in his voice and says, 'Come on! You're on! You're on stage now!'

It's like a bungee jump. There is a mad scramble to get out of the dressing room and into the wings, Penny hopping about trying to get her high heels on. And then we are thrown into the limelight. God knows what this audience of high profile actors and celebrities thinks as we go into our routine – especially the Americans. Miraculously, the lost lines come back to me, and we get to the end of our sketch. Mark gets the Best Light Entertainment programme award and, with a rictus grin on his face, mutely shakes a fist at us on receiving it, as if to say, 'you rascals.'

Our appearance is over in maybe less than one minute. We head for the Green Room and Bar. There is a huge monitor to the left of the door and lined up at the bar watching it are the well-known actors waiting to be called to present an award. We get a drink and line up with them, staring at the monitor. And then a tall, exquisitely attired man in dark glasses enters, stands directly in front of TV monitor facing the celebrities, removes his dark glasses, smiles confidently and says, 'Good evening.' Twinkle in his eye. This man is sending the event up. And then I recognise him. It is the handsome Rock Hudson. The celebrities stare at him impassively. He shrugs nonchalantly and steps away from the enormous television monitor. I could see he had humour combined with style.

John Alderton loses Best Actor Award to Edward Woodward as Callan.

The award ceremony ends with Best Music for the film *Z* to Mikis Theodorakis, well-known for his *Zorba the Greek* theme, a prolific composer of traditional, classical and popular music. A Greek man collects the award on his behalf, saying that the composer cannot be here to collect the award because he is in prison. There is a laugh from the gallery. Annoyed, the recipient of the Theodorakis award says something about it not being funny, because the composer opposes the current regime in Greece for which he is imprisoned and may be tortured. The award ceremony ends on that note and the end credits roll.

The BAFTA Awards are not live but will be transmitted an hour later. I head back to Highgate in a taxi to watch it. On the way, I think about the events in Greece. In the late sixties a right-wing junta of military colonels took over the country and many left-wing liberals opposing the regime were imprisoned. There was no freedom in Greece until 1974 when the regime was overthrown. During the ruling of the military colonels, Theodorakis's music was banned.

A cast read-through at LWT's Station House for the film, in the week prior to the start of the shoot. It was great to hear some of Esmonde and Larbey's best lines being spoken. My favourite being Norman Potter's and Mrs Abbott's after she has seen her 'little soldier' on to the coach for the summer camp. As though in great pain, Barbara Mitchell clutches her breast and says, 'They had to do away with my fallopians when I gave birth to Frankie, you know.' To which Potter replies, 'Kept jumping on the pram, did they?'

John and Bob's script got loads of laughs. Following the read-through, everyone was in a jubilant mood as we headed for the bar on the twentieth floor. We were introduced to Carol Hawkins, our new Sharon, replacing Penny who turned down the role. Carol was a new face to me but is someone who has also been busy in the business since then, appearing in several *Carry*

THE RANK ORGANISATION PRESENTS
An L.W.I. Production – Leslie Grade Film
JOHN ALDERTON in **PLEASE SIR!**
with DERYCK GUYLER · JOAN SANDERSON · NOEL HOWLETT
Hear CILLA BLACK Sing "LA, LA, LA, LU"

On films, and many other television shows. And I later discovered in talking to her that not long before being offered the *Please Sir!* film she trained at Corona Academy. But the cast of the film read-through, unlike a television rehearsal, was enormous, and we barely had a chance to get to know her on that first day.

Nobody really knows why Penny turned down the part. Mark was desperate to cast her. Peter Cleall has since told me that Mark asked him to contact Penny to see if he could persuade her to accept the role. Peter protested to the producer that they were only girlfriend and boyfriend in the script, not in real life. But Mark was insistent, so Peter telephoned Penny and asked her why she wouldn't appear in the film. According to Peter, all she replied was, 'Well, there you go, man.'

(I asked Penny about this when I interviewed her at the Phoenix Artist Club in April 2017, and she said one of the reasons she turned down the part was because she was becoming broody, but I suspected wacky-backy also had something to do with it.)

Shooting began early on the Monday morning in the district of Primrose Hill. This was the scene on the zebra crossing where we hold up the traffic. Although this was one of the early opening title scenes, it didn't mean the film was necessarily being shot in sequence. It was simply that during the first week all the London exterior scenes were shot before we went to Pinewood Studios for the interior classroom scenes, and various other interiors.

If you watch old British films, especially B-movies, you will see Eden's Removal lorries in the background of many location shots. This was because the removal firm was often used to ferry props and equipment to various film locations, and sneakily let their vehicles be seen in the back of many shots, giving them free advertising. Eden's was used for *Please, Sir!* and Pat Kelly, our first assistant director, was often beside himself as he shouted, 'That fucking Eden's van is in the back of every fucking shot. Get rid of the fucking Eden's van.'

Years later, Zélie and I attended a Lowry exhibition at the Royal Academy. After his mother died, Lowry attended his first London exhibition, and painted scenes of the capital. One of the exhibits we saw that day at the Royal Academy was called *On Location,* a painting of a film scene, and in the background of the painting an Eden's van was discernible. I imagined Pat Kelly standing over Lowry as he painted the scene, yelling, 'Get rid of that fucking Eden's van.'

After only four lessons, I passed my driving test. Because Peter Cleall lived in Brighton, he occasionally stayed at our flat in Highgate. We had a lot more room now as about a year prior to starting the third series, we had moved to a large unfurnished flat a little further down the hill in Hornsey Lane, and handily opposite The Old Crown pub.

It was always an early start, and I drove us to Pinewood in the tiny Austin A40. I also gave Liz a lift, as she lived close by at Kentish Town. Whenever we arrived at the studio gates in my baby Austin, the commissionaire saluted us with deadpan irony.

At Pinewood Studio we could relax, mainly because we could lounge around our spacious dressing rooms while waiting to be called. It also gave us an opportunity to get to know Carol better. Malcolm was in a West End play, *Forget-Me-Not Lane* by Peter Nichols, which I had seen him performing at Greenwich Theatre prior to its West End transfer. It meant Malcolm had to dash off at the end of every shooting day and had to wear a terrible wig. As his play was set in the 1940s, his hair had to be cut short.

One of the early interior scenes that was shot at Pinewood was the assembly scene where 5C get out of hand and cause a riot. A small boy, dying to go to the loo, wriggles uncomfortably. When Smithy notices and excuses him, he also notices that he is too late, and there is a puddle on the floor where the boy stood. The small boy was an uncredited role played by Todd Carty, who went on to star as Peter 'Tucker' Jenkins in *Grange Hill* and *Tucker's Luck*.

Following the business of the small boy peeing on the floor, we see in the next section two youngsters snogging, then a non-speaking teacher, played by Joan Sanderson's husband, Gregory Scott, comes and drags them out of the line, without first registering that he has seen them as if he has eyes in the back of his head.

For our classroom scenes, Peter Cleall added a political message in chalk on the blackboard which can be seen behind John Alderton's shots. The message reads: 'Hands Off Our Milk!' This was a reference to Margaret Thatcher, who was Minister of Education at the time and she abolished free school milk, becoming known as 'Mrs Thatcher the Milk Snatcher!'

I can't remember where the road was where we shot the scenes in the coach heading for the summer camp. Presumably, it must have been reasonably close to the studio, and a quiet road. The frustrated coach driver was played by Jack Smethurst who played the bigoted Eddie Booth in the controversial television comedy *Love They Neighbour* which ran for seven series between 1972 and 1976. Incredible when you think how outlawed such questionable humour is in today's climate.

Although we had all left school by the end of the third series, and Bernard Hedges and Penny Wheeler married in the final episode, the film ignored any television continuity and the two of them meet for the first time in unfavourable circumstances because the mischievous Wesley pretends to Penny that Hedges is a racist. Wesley was played by Brinsley Forde, who played Spring in the children's television series *Here Come the Double Deckers* and went on to become lead singer of the phenomenally successful British reggae band Aswad.

In the studio bar one evening, we were introduced to a smooth man, probably in his late thirties, wearing a

40

shiny mohair suit. His name was Barry Gout, and my first impression of him was one of deep distrust. He looked like a used car salesman, a man who could sling you a line and sell you a duff motor. And sling us a line he did. He told us he was a record producer and wanted us to record a *Please Sir!* single. He also said, 'I could make each of you kids a couple of thou easily.' We fell for his patter and found ourselves in a recording studio late one night after filming. The recording session had to be late because of Malcolm's commitment in *Forget-Me-Not Lane.*

The 'Please Sir!' song on the A-side was written by M. McFee and H. Rabinowitz. Harry Rabinowitz was more of a classical music conductor, and was Head of Music at LWT, and conducted the London Symphony and Royal Philharmonic Orchestras during a long and distinguished career. God knows why he got involved in writing a mediocre record like the one we recorded, when tempers were stretched to breaking point.

It soon became clear to us that Barry Gout had little experience as a record producer. Most of what he did in the studio that night was to heap encouragement on us and ply us with beer. By the time we got to record the B-side, not only were we shattered, having been up since 5.30 a.m. to get to the studio for a day's filming, but we were also getting quite tipsy. And we would be lucky to get three hours sleep, as we were called for filming the next day. The B-side was called 'Life, Life, Life' and was written by T. Parker, M. McFee, P. Denyer.

I can remember Peter Cleall criticising the song (rightly, I think) as a dirge, which didn't go down well with Peter Denyer. Malcolm was a bit more sanguine, probably accepting that it was merely a B-side. The song was carelessly rushed, as not only were we exhausted, we were in a terrible mood. It was a relief to grab a taxi and get home to bed for a few hours' sleep.

After the record was released, it didn't sell many copies, and we heard that Barry Gout was in trouble because none of the session musicians got paid, and the record producer did a bunk.

The camp scenes in the film were shot in Black Park, a forest not far from Pinewood, which has often been used for locations when rural scenes are required. They built prefabricated huts, in which we could also shoot interior scenes in the camp.

Mark Stuart had less temper tantrums during the filming than when he was in the television studio. I guess that's because filming has a slower pace than television, giving actors and directors time to rehearse while the cinematographer lights each scene. Our director of photography was Wilkie

41

Cooper, who also photographed *Seven Waves Away* (U.S. title *Abandon* Ship) a 1956 film set in a civilian lifeboat in the South Atlantic, starring Tyrone Power and Mai Zetterling, and in which I played Peter Kilgore. And the South Atlantic was played by Shepperton Studios Sound Stage.

Mark did, however, lose his temper during the filming of one scene when we were playing football, and he grabbed an extra by the scruff of the neck. Perhaps the poor benighted lad was talking while Mark gave direction. It was a disturbing scene to witness, and Mark came close to seriously assaulting the young man.

There was a scene where we are all in the dining room, including 5C's enemies from the rival Weaver Street School. In the scene, Eric Duffy overhears one of the Weaver Street kids taking the mickey out of Dennis. He then walks over and shoves a jam tart in the face of the pupil, played by Richard Everett. I was sitting next to Peter, we were chatting about something and not concentrating. Suddenly we heard Mark shout 'Action!' I could see by the look in Peter's eyes that he was unclear whether this was a rehearsal or a take. He had two options, rehearsal or a take. He quickly tossed a metaphorical coin in his head and chose the latter. He carried the jam tart over to Richard Everett, and said threateningly, 'Did you say something, you pasty-faced pillock?' Then let him have it with the jam tart. Jam trickled all over the shocked actor's face, down his neck and over his school uniform. 'Cut!' Mark yelled. Then growled, 'That was a rehearsal.'

The actor then had to go to make-up and wardrobe to get cleaned up and put on a new uniform. This was one instance where Mark, strangely enough, didn't go berserk. He even suppressed a smile, knowing, probably, how stupid Peter must have felt. Later, Richard Everett told us he thought Peter had lost the plot.

Towards the end of one shooting week, we all had a night out at Danny La Rue's Club in Hanover Square. It started off as a great night out, with Danny La Rue making jokes about the Fenn Street Gang, but after a week of getting up at the crack of dawn, and filming all day until six every evening, we were all knackered. After a few drinks, eyelids started to close, and we soon became zombies.

I might be wrong, but I seem to remember that the last scene that was shot in the film was the final party scene, with us dancing along to Tony Orlando and Dawn singing 'Knock Three Times'. We had yet to hear the number that would be used in the final edit and post-production.

Usually post-production on a film back then would have taken the best part of a year. Maybe Mark worked hard with editor Richard Best because the film was released by November. We all attended the first showing at the Victoria Metropole Cinema, where we heard for the first time Cilla Black singing 'La, La, La, Lu' for the party scene.

It has been suggested to me that if anyone wants to get full enjoyment from the last scene in the film, drag out your old Sony Walkman, stick a cassette of 'Knock Three Times' into it, and watch the dancing confident that the movements of the actors will be coordinated with the song. Not that I was uncoordinated. I was too busy stuffing my face with cream cakes.

When the film came out on general release, it got a fantastic reception, with long queues of youngsters waiting to get into their local cinemas during the school holidays and photographs of our characters and stills from the film were printed in hundreds of local newspapers all over the country.

And so many people commented that the film was one of the better TV spin-offs into film.

The Fenn Street Gang

It wasn't long after the release of the film when we began rehearsals for *The Fenn Street Gang* spin-off. Six of us were contracted to appear in 16 out of 21 episodes which ran consecutively with the fourth series of *Please Sir!* Class 5C was recast with other young actors playing different characters, the school keeper and staff were the same, except for Glyn Edwards who played Richard Dix for two episodes, a new 5C teacher called David Ffitchett-Brown, played by Richard Warwick, and Mr Hurst played by Bernard Holley for eight episodes.

Now John and Bob's writing was put to the test. Of the first series of 21 episodes of *Fenn Street Gang*, they wrote 11 episodes, and of the 21 episodes of series four of *Please Sir!* they wrote eight episodes, plus working as script editors on the other scripts for both series. Two of *The Fenn Street Gang* and five episodes of the new *Please Sir!* were written by Tony Bilbow, who presented BBC Television's *Film Night* between 1970 and 1973, and Geoff Rowley and Andy Baker wrote seven episodes of *Please Sir!* and seven of *Fenn Street Gang*. I wrote one episode of the latter.

Mark Stuart, as executive producer was still in charge of both series, but we now had other alternating producers and directors. We still had Alan Wallis, who had directed us on series three of *Please Sir!*, and we also had David Askey, Philip Casson, Howard Ross, Graham Evans and Bryan Izzard.

John Alderton was contracted to appear in two episodes of the new school series and three episodes of *The Fenn Street Gang*. Malcolm McFee was unavailable to continue as Peter Craven because the production company, Memorial Enterprises, wouldn't release him from his West End play. He had an understudy, and only one week after our series started, they gave notice that the play would finish in two weeks. You would have thought that a production company run by two actors, Albert Finney and Michael Medwin, would have been understanding and let Malcolm go before the end, since the end was imminent, and Malcolm would lose out on a 16-episode series.

But no, they insisted on him staying until the final curtain, even though his understudy could have played the part for the last two weeks. Léon Vitali was cast as Peter Craven

The first episode, *Should Auld Acquaintance,* was not a happy memory. Nothing to do with any aggravation with the cast or production. It was directed by David Askey and on the second day, when producer Mark Stuart came into the rehearsal room to watch a rehearsal, he seemed to be staring at me which I misinterpreted as his dissatisfaction with my performance. At the end of a scene, he came forward, took me by the shoulders, saying he wanted a word with me, and I was taken into an adjoining empty rehearsal room. He then told me he had bad news. My brother, Mervyn, had died in Australia.

My first inappropriate thought was relief that I wasn't being sacked. This terrible immediate thought has filled me with such guilt that I have been unable to wash it away. It has haunted me ever since.

When I look back at that first episode, I think how kind and understanding Mark was. He took me into his office, then left me to telephone Zélie, who told me Jenny, Mervyn's wife, would be ringing me later that evening from Australia. We broke for lunch and I went home early.

The cause of Mervyn's death was pleurisy, which is not usually life-threatening, but Mervyn had been in an extremely bad motor accident a year before they immigrated to Australia. He spent over six weeks in hospital, and I guess his body had weakened considerably and was unable to cope with the viral infection.

The next few days were a blur, and I suppose a sort of 'Doctor Theatre'[1] got me through the recording. Everyone was supportive and understanding. The first episode was written by John and Bob and opened with us playing tenpin bowls. Christopher Biggins was in this episode, as a Royal Mail employee. He had a scene with Peter Craven, now played by Léon Vitali. I felt sorry for Léon, because he was thrown in at the deep end, and they had obviously cast him on his looks, whereas he never really nailed the character, because there wasn't really a big enough contrast between him and Peter Cleall. It wasn't Léon's fault, he just played it differently to Malcolm, who had been laid-back and understood the art of more is less. But as Sharon, Carol Hawkins, although different from Penny Spencer, managed to take the character to another level and succeeded in making it her own.

I guess I managed to get through these early episodes because I was kept busy and didn't have time to dwell on Mervyn's death. Besides, by then more than five years had passed since he had left the UK and the move had placed a vast distance between us. The wrench at the time already felt like a bereavement, never knowing when we might meet again, and never suspecting that we never would.

The second episode, *The Start of Something Big*, written by Rowley and Baker, featured Christopher Timothy, with whom we would become involved over the next few years. This was the episode in which we are introduced to Duffy's painting and decorating workmate played by Mike Grady, who appeared in several episodes as Batch, another rather dense cheeky chappie. Mike was excellent in *Citizen Smith* as Robert Lindsay's mate Ken, a John Sullivan series which became hugely popular from 1977 to 1980.

But during his stint as Batch I can remember Mark complaining to whoever directed one of those particular episodes that Rowley and Baker's writing wasn't working as far as Mike's characterization was concerned as he was being written as too similar in style to Frankie Abbott.

In the fourth episode, *Horses for Courses*, Terry Duggan was again our barman in The Feathers, as he had been in Episode One. Married to Anna Karen, who was working at the time as Olive in *On the Buses*, we often bumped into her and the cast in the LWT bar. Sally Thomsett, looking incredibly young, having played a child in *The Railway Children* film at the age of twenty, was also in this episode, playing a Scottish young woman who confuses Dennis.

1   In the acting profession, if someone is ill, or sprains an ankle badly, but is still able to perform without a member of the audience noticing that anything is wrong, this coping mechanism is known as 'Dr Theatre'.

David Askey, who directed this episode, had just become a father and wasn't getting much sleep. In this episode Craven smashes his GPO motor bike and enlists Duffy's help to get rid of it in the river – Abbott tags along with a commando blacked-up face. It was quite a long night sequence, finishing the shoot in the early hours. We were called to rehearse the next episode, *Meet the Wizard,* only nine hours after we completed the night shoot. Everyone was shattered when we met to begin at noon. Especially David Askey. Bags under his eyes. Face like a cadaver.

But John Alderton was bright-eyed, full of energy and showing deep dissatisfaction with the scripts, even going to see Cyril Bennett, the programme controller at one stage and demanding rewrites. Especially *Meet the Wizard,* penned by Rowley and Baker, where Bernard Hedges is unemployed, and the Labour Exchange finds him work without telling him what the job is or who it's for. And then, even more unbelievably, he finds himself working alongside Frankie Abbott at the Webber and Barlow detective agency. This is after he meets Craven and his mate, played by Robin Askwith, at the Labour Exchange. Hedges gets a job demonstrating a food mixer, which goes horribly wrong. Later Robin Askwith, who would go on to star as Timmy Lea in the hugely successful *Confessions* film franchise, becomes the demonstrator, and we get food splattered all over the store again.

There was a scene at the end of this episode, a domestic between Bernard and Penny. John suddenly announced that the scene wasn't working. I could feel David Askey thinking: *Here we go again.* Then John pointed to me and said, 'I think David should be in this scene.'

John began to argue with the director, who was in no shape to deal with it. And when Askey rightly pointed out that there was no reason for me to be there, John insisted on getting the script altered to make allowances for my inclusion in the scene. David Askey's reaction: zilch. The director had bailed out. Abnegated responsibility. Zombie-like he sat at his director's table, head cupped in hands, probably fantasising about sleeping in a comfortable bed with no baby to wake him.

I always got on well with John, and I know he liked my character, which was perhaps why he wanted me in the scene. And he knew the scene would work so much better with me sitting between him and Jill Kerman on the sofa, feeling excruciatingly embarrassed by this verbal tennis match. John got his own way, the final scene was rewritten, as a result I ended up with the tagline for the episode.

John Alderton's last of his five contracted episodes was very strange. Even though it was under the banner of *The Fenn Street Gang,* not one of the gang appeared in it, the main players being John, Jill Kerman and Wanda Ventham, and it had nothing to do with the Gang.

There was a rumour doing the rounds (I didn't know whether it was true or not) that the only reason John agreed to do the five episodes was if LWT would bury his sitcom character by contracting him for a drama series, which turned out to be *Upstairs, Downstairs* in which he played Thomas the chauffeur. If this rumour was true then it was a very smart move on his or his agent's part, because the *Upstairs, Downstairs* series eventually led to the spin-off *Thomas and Sarah* in which he played opposite his wife, Pauline Collins. They also played husband and wife in the situation comedy *No, Honestly.*

Tony Bilbow only wrote two episodes of *Fenn Street*, neither of which I appeared in. One of these was called *Distant Horizons,* and Sharon's mother was played by Barbara Keogh. Why they hadn't cast Diana Coupland, who was in the first series of *Please Sir!* as Mrs Eversleigh I have no idea. The dates of our show didn't clash with the recording of her performance as Sid James's wife in *Bless This House.* But maybe her fee now was too demanding for the LWT budget? They cast Barbara Keogh instead, who became really well-known in 1998 when she spent a year playing Lilly Mattock in *EastEnders.* I liked Barbara a great deal and I thought she brought extra emphasis to the role of Sharon's mother, although in rehearsals I often slipped away from her presence as she could talk the hind legs off that proverbial donkey.

My next episode, number eight, was written by John and Bob and it was one of my favourites, and it was always their episodes I liked. It was called *The Thin Yellow Line* and was about Abbott joining the army, with Tony Selby as the corporal. Graham Evans directed this episode, and for some reason became annoyed by one of the actors and bullied him. Royce Mills who played the Commanding Officer was his bone of contention and on the first day of rehearsal, as Mills spoke in his terribly, terribly upper-class voice, Evans told him to play it straight and not as a silly toff. Unfortunately, this was Mills' natural voice. There are some actors who can do various accents and voice changes, but clearly Mills wasn't one of them, and Evans became aggressive as he kept stopping Mills every time he opened his mouth, demanding that he play it straight. We were all hugely embarrassed and wondered why Evans took against him so. When I spoke to Liz about it, we both agreed, that a toff's voice was perfect casting for the C.O., especially as this was a comedy.

The second day of rehearsal, Royce Mills was gone and had been replaced by Colin Farrell. I had already worked with Colin, as had Peter Denyer, in *Zigger Zagger*. In case you are thinking this is the Colin Farrell who was in *Ballykissangel*, who went on to Hollywood stardom, think again. Every actor who is an Equity member has their name registered, so that no one else can use their name. Perhaps Colin Farrell the Hollywood star never joined Equity, and refused to change his name, and so it is the Colin Farrell I knew who has had to alter his name to avoid confusion and has now registered his name with Equity as Col Farrell.

Much was made of the fact that my hair was shorn for this episode and, in the opening scenes before I enlisted, I had to wear a wig. One of the filmed sequences took place on army ground, and many squaddies hung around watching. One of the scenes was target practice, in which Abbott gets over-excited by his fantasy of firing a real gun coming true and runs along the firing range shooting from the hip at the target. After Graham Evans shouted 'Cut!', I held the barrel of the rifle. Having never fired a rifle before, and nobody having told me the barrel of a gun gets red hot after firing so many rounds, I yelled and dropped the rifle, blowing on my hands.

The squaddies fell about and most of them commented, 'What a wanker!'

And I had just given them conclusive evidence that David Barry really was like Frankie Abbott!

One of the joys of working in this episode was because Barbara Mitchell was in it, and her character was now going from strength to strength, especially when she became a wheelchair user in one scene, grieving for the loss of 'her little soldier' who really *has* become a little soldier. She was so funny in this particular episode, I often found it difficult not to corpse. Barbara being tall and striking looking, much taller than me, meant that the contrast in our heights was a great look for comedy.

I was lucky that the next two episodes I appeared in were written by John and Bob, *These Foolish Things* and *Kill or Cure,* in which Janina Faye, also an ex-Corona Academy student, reappeared as Hermione (she played a young Conservative in the *Please Sir!* episode *Catch a Falling Dropout*). In 1961, as a child actor, Janina starred as Helen Keller in *The Miracle Worker* at Wyndham's Theatre in the West End and appeared in the 1958 Hammer Horror *Dracula* with Peter Cushing.

Another young Conservative in this episode was Christopher Mitchell as Edgar. Chris was a really lovely bloke, and I got on well with him, as most people did. He played Gunner Parky in *It Ain't Half Hot Mum*. His father,

Norman Mitchell was an actor, and he appeared in the *Fenn Street* episode *From Sudbury With Love*. Sadly, Christopher Mitchell died from cancer in 2001, just a month before his father died.

It was around this time things became hectic as not only did we appear in our own series, but we also had to double rehearse for *The Old Fennians*, an episode of *Please Sir!* series four, although Peter Cleall and Liz had already appeared in one episode each of the new series. *The Old Fennians* was written by Tony Bilbow in which 5C return to their old school for a reunion, and we get to meet the new 5C played by Billy Hamon, Charles Bolton, Barry McCarthy, Drina Pavlovic and Rosemary Faith. They were very friendly, although working on two series at the same time, we barely had time to get to know them. We had seen some episodes of the of the fourth series, and all of us old 5C actors agreed that Charles Bolton as Godber gave an excruciatingly unreal performance. And it was probably not the fault of the other actors, more to do with the writing, but their characters were not so well defined, and some of their lines could have been interchangeable. The two young women came out of the new series best, as their characters were more defined, and this was one of the reasons I would cast Rosemary Faith as my girlfriend in *One For The Pot* in years to come. But I found performing in this episode of series four a trifle embarrassing. It was written by Tony Bilbow, and I wished his parents had never given him a pen and pencil set one Christmas.

Quite early in the *Fenn Street* series I thought about Abbott's relationship with his overbearing mother and wondered what might have happened to the character's father. I wrote about it in a synopsis, with some scene and dialogue examples, and gave it to John and Bob. They liked it and I was commissioned to write the script, which I called *When Did You Last See Your Father?* It was broadcast on Christmas Eve.

In this episode Abbott, who has been lied to by his mother and thinks his father might be a top secret spy, discovers he works as a lowly clerk in a labour exchange. Little did I think in 1971 that I would be appearing as a 70-year-old Abbott in a care home, creating a poignant scene in which he recalls seeing his father at the Labour Exchange, in a play at the Edinburgh Fringe Festival in 2016.

The next episode in the TV series was *A Fair Swap*, written by Rowley and Baker, in which the Gang for some strange reason get caught up in a medical student rag. It was directed by the flamboyant and camp Bryan Izzard, was quite manic, and ended with a shot of a street sign called Droop Street. No doubt it tickled the director when he saw it, and thought he would throw it in, even though the street postcode was W10, a long way from the gang's East End.

In the bar we often tried to persuade Mark Stuart to let John and Bob write an episode where we all go on a day trip to Calais or Boulogne. The nearest we got to a French day trip was an episode in which we all go to Brighton, called *The Clean Weekend*.

During the day's shoot, I think Alan Wallis who directed this episode got a little concerned as everyone's wife or girlfriend – and in Peter Cleall's case, his children - joined the party for a day out. It was a wild shoot, and much of what we did was improvised. In one scene, we were playing football on the beach, and the ball ended up being swept out to sea on the outgoing tide. Someone grabbed a rowing boat, then Peter Cleall and one of the technical crew rowed out after it. The cameraman turned his camera on and shot it. He said if they had an accident and drowned he'd be able to sell the footage to ITN News.

I hoped he was joking, but I was never sure.

Following the rescue of the ball, an irate man turned up claiming it was his boat that had been used and how dare the film crew take it without permission. The production manager bunged him twenty pounds to keep him happy and he left hurriedly. Afterwards, we all wondered whether it really was his boat.

Episode 18, *Horse of the Year*, written by John and Bob, featured James Beck as an auctioneer. Beck played the spiv Private Walker in *Dad's Army* from 1968 until 1973. He was very funny in this episode and he even stuck in a few ad-libs in rehearsals, calling Abbott Jo-Jo the dog-faced boy. John and Bob were never precious about their writing and if someone added something funny into the scene they were quite happy for it to be left in.

I got on extremely well with Jimmy Beck. He was a heavy drinker, but the booze didn't seem to affect his performance in any way. Just his memory. Six weeks after this episode, I happened to be in Gerry's, an actors' club in Shaftesbury Avenue. Sitting at the bar was Jimmy. I went over, tapped him familiarly on the shoulder and said, 'Hi, Jimmy.'

He stared at me coldly, hadn't a clue who I was, and his expression said how dare I presume to be so familiar. Alcoholic amnesia. He died of pancreatitis aged 44 in 1973.

One of Rowley and Baker's more manic episodes was Episode 19, *From Sudbury With Love*, which featured Norman Mitchell as a policeman having an assignation with a female PC in a bus shelter. This was a front cloth spot and had little to do with the episode's plot but was reasonably funny. One of the main characters in the episode was an Italian played by Lynda Bellingham, who became famous as the wife in the 'Oxo Family', playing opposite her Oxo husband, Michael Redfern, with whom I attended Corona Academy many years ago. Bellingham would also appear in over eighty episodes of *All Creatures Great and Small*, when she replaced Carol Drinkwater as James Herriot's wife. And Anthony Morton, who played the Italian Papa in this episode, I had worked with when he was Carlos the Spanish chef in *Crossroads*.

We often had actors playing different roles in either *Please Sir!* or *The Fenn Street Gang*. Alfredo in this episode was played by Roger Carey, who played the Greek nephew of Uncle Niklos in *A Near Greek Tragedy* in the first series of the former. Carey retired from acting and became a successful theatrical agent. The Greek uncle was played by Fred Beauman, who then played a Romany gypsy in the film. And Rosalind Elliott, who would later become Celeste, my girlfriend in the next series, played Gina in this episode, an Italian girl they try to force Frankie to marry.

Having left the army, and no longer working for Ronnie Drew the private detective, played by Neil Wilson, who played a bookmaker in an episode of *Please Sir!*, Abbott works as a waiter in an Italian restaurant, with many unbelievable and over-the-top scenes. Although there was one of these café scenes which was quite funny as Mr Dunstable takes Mrs Abbott out to tea at Frankie's establishment, and tries to woo her by playing the spoons. To watch Barbara Mitchell and Peter Bayliss hamming it up was great fun.

Doctor at Large was being produced by LWT at this time, with Barry Evans, George Layton and my old school friend Richard O'Sullivan. We were at Corona together, and we often used to socialise when we were in the senior students' school, and it was he who managed to get me a good featured role in Walt Disney's *The Prince and The Pauper* because they were three weeks behind on their shooting schedule, and Richard had only played one scene when his contract ran out and he was already signed to do the Cliff Richard film, *The Young Ones*, in which he partnered Melvyn Hayes. As I was doubling for Richard on the Disney film, they offered me the part, and I actually got to meet Walt Disney when he came to Shepperton Studios for the wrap party.

It was great to meet up with Richard again in the LWT bar after so many years had gone by. And I also spotted another actor who I often referred to jokingly as 'Dad'. This was Ralph Michael, who appeared as the Dean in four episodes of *Doctor at Large*. He played my father when I appeared in *Seven Waves Away*, and a year later we toured Europe in *Titus Andronicus*, when he played Bassianus, the emperor's brother. When I said 'hello' to him and called him 'Dad' in the LWT bar, he looked confused until I explained who I was.

The last episode in the *Fenn Street* series *The Great Frock Robbers* was, thankfully, written by John and Bob. In this episode we were introduced to Bowler, a pretentious villain, superbly played by George Baker, with some great lines from the writers.

Not everything had been plain sailing, however. Comedy actor John Junkin did our studio warm-ups. He was fun and entertaining, and the audience seemed to like him because he was a well-known face. He always joined us for a meal after the recording. But his warm-up days were numbered because of the sensitivity of our bosses. It happened during one warm-up, when John Junkin told the audience that LWT stood for 'Low Wages and Tat!' The curtain came down, and for the next episode we had another warm-up man.

The success of the first series which was broadcast from 17 September 1971 until 11 February 1972 assured us of a second series later in the year. Out of 21 weeks, the series spent 14 weeks in the top twenty, and reached a high of Number One with the episode *The Thin Yellow Line*, when Abbott goes into the army.

The South Bank

Malcolm McFee, who couldn't have been more than 22-years-old, became an impresario, when he contacted Theatre Royal Stratford East, not far from where he lived in Forest Gate, and decided to revive *Under Milk Wood* there, but this time a full-scale production using a proper set. Peter Denyer directed the production, and he chose to have many of the characters appearing in windows which lit up. I later discovered this idea was used in the original BBC television production.

Playing the Narrator was Liz's husband Ian, who learnt the marathon part. Christopher Timothy also joined the cast and gave a superbly memorable performance as Organ Morgan. Chris was originally from Bala, North Wales, and lived near Harlow with his family at the time. He often hitch-hiked down the A11 for the evening's performance to save money.

Apart from Ian and Chris, the cast was pretty much the same as our one night at Lewisham, and we played Theatre Royal E.15 for a fortnight. It was during this run that I had an out of body experience. There were some empty seats in the front row of the circle. I was onstage giving my Reverend Eli Jenkins morning prayer speech which starts 'Dear Gwalia!' and all I can remember after that is sitting in the front row of the circle watching myself performing and listening to the speech. I was definitely a member of the audience and not on that stage. At least, that's what it felt like. The speech is not that long, and I returned to my own body as it ended... 'And never, never leave the town.' I was back on stage.

There may be a rational explanation (Buddhists call the experience 'Astral Projection' I believe) but I never personally encountered anything like it before then or since. And I don't think it was like the automatic pilot experience you sometimes get when driving. When I was in the front row of the circle, I was aware of what was happening on stage, even though I wasn't there. I was the observer. It was a novel, even esoteric experience, but far from spooky.

1971 turned out to be quite an eventful year. It was Zélie's turn to be offered a summer season at the Pavilion Theatre Torquay. It was another Sam Cree comedy, with Kenneth Connor, Bernard Bresslaw and Charles Hawtrey topping the bill. During my stint in the Jack Douglas play, Zélie and I had discovered a small out-of-the-way pub which became our bolthole, knowing that no other members of the *Don't Tell Your Wife* company drank there. Prior to starting my next job, I went down to see Zélie's play and spent a week there. One night we were at the bar in our secret pub, and we had been there only a few minutes when who should walk in but Charles Hawtrey, looking exactly like he does in the *Carry On* films. From behind his glasses he looked like a cheeky schoolboy feigning innocence. Hanging from his shoulder was a little blue toggle bag which added to the cute effect. There was something rather sweet about him, almost like a puppy dog wanting to be patted.

'Ooh, hello, Zélie,' he said to my wife. Then, 'Aren't you going to introduce me to your nice young man?'

When I went to buy the actor a drink, he wouldn't hear of it. 'No, you must let me get them,' he insisted, oozing sweetness and light. The landlord and his wife, having recognised Hawtrey, were clearly too embarrassed to ask him for money – a round for which he had conveniently forgotten to pay.

At first, I was fooled by this, as were the publicans, but when I made a move to get the next round, he repeated the ploy, insisting that he wanted to get the drinks. By now it was becoming awkward because the landlord and his wife clearly didn't know how to handle the situation. Hawtrey insisted on getting every single round and didn't once put his hand in his pocket. I felt sorry for the publicans, and I suspected Hawtrey knew damn well what he was doing.

After closing time, he insisted we accompanied him to a club, where he did the same thing, probably knowing he could get away with it by pretending to forget, and confident that people were uneasy about demanding payment from a celebrity. I heard that Charles actually became notorious for this ploy and was regularly banned from local pubs in Deal, the seaside town he moved to in 1968 and died in twenty years later.

Around December the previous year, the Queens Theatre in Hornchurch offered me the part of Young Frank in *Forget-Me-Not Lane*. This was the play I had seen, which featured Malcolm playing Ivor, Young Frank's friend, at Greenwich Theatre before it transferred to the West End. I loved the play and didn't hesitate to accept the role. The post West End tour of the play was produced by Bill Kenwright, with Davy Jones of the Monkees playing Young Frank. Prior to my Hornchurch engagement, Bill contacted my agent and asked if I would take over from Davy Jones for one week at Weston-Super-Mare, because for some reason the singer had to dash back to the U.S. for that week. On a Tuesday I picked up a copy of the script at Kenwright's office, then the next day I travelled to Bournemouth where the play was currently performing. Playing the leads in the cast were Dave King as Frank, a comedian who long ago starred in his own television shows, and the father was played by Edward Chapman, particularly known as the long-suffering Mr Grimsdale from the Norman Wisdom films. Tom Owen played Ivor and Young Ursula was played by Wendy Padbury from *Crossroads*.

When I got to Bournemouth, I spent every waking moment learning the lines. I would walk along the street muttering them, getting weird looks from people. The rehearsal time I was allocated wasn't enough. The cast was reluctant to devote more than a few hours a day as they had to perform the show every night and twice on Saturday. I had to make do with remote and intensive line learning, catching an hour here or there with some of the more obliging members of the cast, and of course I watched the show every night. I occasionally bumped into Davy Jones if he stayed for a drink in the bar afterwards, and he was very polite when we had a brief chat, but otherwise we had little contact as there was no need for him to rehearse.

One of the major obstacles was working with Edward Chapman who was an alcoholic. We had a dress rehearsal for my benefit on Friday morning, and this was only my third day in Bournemouth. In one scene Chapman entered not knowing where he was, having cut something like ten pages. David Buck, the director, stopped him, saying with as much patience as he could muster, 'Ted, you're two scenes too early.'

Confused, Chapman paused. You could see his fuddled brain trying to grasp at clues for which scene or what play he was in. Then, clearly deciding attack was the best form of defence, he cursed the stage management. 'Well, why can't that girl set the props in the correct place?' he yelled.

It was a shabby way to transfer the blame and everyone felt embarrassed.

When I got home that weekend, I spent the entire time going over the lines, drumming them into my head. When I arrived at Weston-Super-Mare on Monday, I saw my name was emblazoned across the front of the theatre. Dave King went berserk because his contract with Kenwright gave him top billing. It led to a heated argument with the manager, and I later discovered the change of billing may have been because King had upset Weston-Super-

Mare audiences in the past. Having died a death at the venue, as the curtain came down one night he told them to 'Piss off!'

Eventually, because it looked as if Dave King was not going to back down and refused to go on stage unless the billing was changed, John Ingram, the company manager, came into my dressing room and asked if I would mind if the billing was changed.

'I couldn't care less if you take my name off completely,' I said carelessly. 'Because I'm only here for a week.'

Having seen the excellent pre-West End production at Greenwich, I didn't tell him how disillusioned I was with this production. The billing was changed and the play opened. There were a few mistakes but nothing major. I got through it, despite Edward Chapman's erratic entrances and exits, and the scenes I most enjoyed were with Tom Owen and Wendy Padbury. But by Saturday I was relieved it was over. Apart from my scenes with Tom and Wendy, the production had been a huge disappointment.

After the curtain fell on Saturday night, I said goodbye to the cast. I didn't want to bear a grudge and part bad company with Edward Chapman, so I entered his dressing room to say goodbye. 'Would you like a drink for the road, son?' he offered, clearly trying to make amends for any shortcomings in his performance during the week. I was puzzled. Where was the booze? He was barred from bringing it into the theatre. My eyes quickly scanned the dressing table but I saw no alcohol. He then picked up a shampoo bottle with amber liquid inside. 'It's whisky,' he whispered, glancing furtively over his shoulder. I declined the drink, explaining that I had a long drive ahead.

Soon after, I began rehearsals at Hornchurch, one of the most relaxed rehearsal periods I can ever remember. I already knew the lines and could enjoy the in-depth exploration of the play, and not go home every evening to learn lines. This production was far superior to the Kenwright tour. The cast worked as a team, with everyone pulling their weight, and when it opened the audiences laughed uproariously at every funny line.

A few weeks after the Hornchurch production, another phone call to my agent from Kenwright's office. Davy Jones was returning to America for the final two weeks of the tour. Would I take over? No way, I said. I emphatically did not want to be involved in this production. Bill must have guessed my reason for turning it down and reassured my agent that Edward Chapman had been replaced by James Hayter, and everything now ran smoothly.

James Hayter was in *Seven Waves Away,* my first film, and when I worked backstage at Drury Lane in *My Fair Lady* during my student days, he played

Doolittle. He struck me as a lovely man and very professional. Thinking nothing could go wrong now, I accepted the two-week engagement. Big mistake. Probably one of the biggest of my career.

Davy Jones's final week was at the Ashcroft Theatre, Croydon, and I joined the cast on the Friday to be rehearsed into it. Despite knowing the lines, the moves of the actors would be slightly different to the Hornchurch production. After becoming reacquainted with James Hayter, rehearsals began. It was then I discovered there had been a coup and Dave King now controlled John Ingram and everyone in the company.

'We've changed some of the lines,' Dave King said. Meaning *he* had changed the lines. Because he came from somewhere east of London, and was unable to portray a Bristolian, Peter Nichols' wonderfully evocative script no longer conjured up images of Frank's commercial traveller father as he travels from Yeovil to Minehead but wanders instead to Southend and Basildon. Essex man had brought it closer to home.

'By all means change your lines,' I said. 'But I would sooner stick to Peter Nichols' script. I don't mind what you say, but I'm sticking to the script.'

After this little speech, an Arctic wind blew into the theatre. If I stuck to the script then clearly others in the cast would have to, otherwise none of it would make sense. We broke for coffee and there followed a huddled discussion between John Ingram and Dave King. When the rehearsal resumed, King agreed that we could still set it in the west country – which was big of him, since he hadn't written the play – but he would have to insist, he said, on one of my lines being changed, the one where I talk about a 'woman's minge'. He said many people walked out of the audience when they heard that line. 'So, it's got to be changed, son.'

I asked him what I should change it to, and he told me to say 'woman's thingee' instead. I agreed, and we carried on rehearsing. But I could tell he really hated me now. And he had never once, I noticed, called me by name. It was always 'son' in a condescending, sneering manner.

The following week at Bath Theatre Royal, the tour from hell began. Admittedly it was only for two weeks, but I could imagine if I was really bad in this life, my everlasting punishment would be working for eternity with Dave King.

At Hornchurch I always got a laugh on a certain line, but in Bath the silence that followed was because of Dave King's sudden move behind me as he deliberately killed my line. I didn't know what I could do about this. Then on Wednesday night's performance, hatred struck in a big way. About to deliver the 'woman's thingee' line, a slight hesitation on my part, and then 'minge' inadvertently slipped back into the dialogue.

Cut to my dressing room in the interval. John Ingram asked me to put 'thingee' back in. I explained about it being a mistake because I knew the lines from the Hornchurch version, which was, after all, Peter Nichols' scripted lines.

Suddenly, the dressing room door flew open and in barged King. 'You,' he yelled, doing a lot of finger waving, 'are fucking deliberately ruining everything I'm trying to do on stage.'

I explained that it was a mistake, but it was a waste of time. He was in an abusive mood and looking for trouble.

'You are fucking useless,' he screamed and began to exit.

Perhaps it was a mistake to have the last word but I was damned if I was going to let him get away with that. 'That's the trouble with allowing red-nosed comics into the legitimate theatre,' I said.

Which was unfair and untrue about comedians and variety artistes. But this was a fight. And in fights you have to go for where it hurts the most. Unfortunately, although I am not a moral coward, I'm not the bravest person when confronted by fisticuffs.

Fists clenched, he spun round and came towards me. 'I'll smash your fucking head in, you little cunt.'

I remember thinking at the time that if this was the man who thought nothing of having a go at Lew Grade, managing director of ATV, then he wouldn't hold back on pummelling me. Fortunately, John Ingram stepped between us. I froze, like you do when a savage dog threatens you, having made a split-second decision that if I did nothing, received a blow, the play would be cancelled, resulting in a major lawsuit.

Perhaps he realized this. Without saying another word, he stormed out. The adrenaline pumped through my body, tears sprang into my eyes and I began to shake. John Ingram did his best to calm me down, but as I had been threatened with physical assault I was within my rights to leave the show, I told him. After tonight's performance I was on my way home.

We were called for Act Two. I had to stand by in the wings, and when I got there, Dave King also stood by, a smug, self-satisfied look on his face, the trace of an evil smile. If it was done deliberately to wind me up, it succeeded. I was suddenly so enraged, I went over to him, grabbed his wrist and held it over his head.

'What are you doing,' he snarled, snatching back his hand.

'Congratulations!' I said. 'You wanted to upset me, and you succeeded.'

He made a move towards me. 'I've a good mind to smash your fucking head in.'

The curtain began to rise on Act Two. I backed away. 'OK,' I whispered. 'Cool it. Cool it.'

His upper lip curled angrily. 'Don't start that jazz talk with me, son.'

After the performance, I phoned my agent at his home, told him about the incident, and said I was leaving the show. First thing in the morning I intended driving home. He sympathised with me but asked me to wait until he'd had a word with Kenwright.

The following morning Bill phoned me at the Garrick's Head, where we were staying. He was supportive and told me he wanted to 'get rid of that fucker' but couldn't find anyone to replace him. He pleaded with me to stay with the show, especially as it was only another week and a half to go. Reluctantly, I agreed.

When I got to the theatre that night, James Hayter was also supportive. 'If I was a younger man,' he said, 'I'd have kicked that cunt down the stairs for you.'

For the rest of the run there was a terrible atmosphere. Dave King and I never had to look at one another on stage, as I was playing his younger self. That was a blessing I suppose. But whenever we passed each other backstage, we both avoided eye contact. We hated each other. In fact, I've never known anything like that much hatred between two performers before or since.

The final week at the Yvonne Arnaud Theatre, Guildford, couldn't come quickly enough. And throughout that final week we still avoided eye contact and each other. And then I was slightly cheered up by a form of petty revenge, provided by courtesy of Tom Owen.

Bill arranged to visit the penultimate performance and take the cast out for a meal afterwards to an Italian restaurant. King asked Tom if everyone was dressing for it, and Tom told him, yes, it was the works, black tie do.

I was delighted to see Bill arrive on Friday evening wearing a denim jacket. I almost punched the air jubilantly. And everyone else was casually dressed. The only one feeling more than a little over-dressed at dinner was Dave King, wearing a dinner jacket, black bow tie and horrendously over-the-top frilly shirt.

Yes, I thought. *A vengeance of sorts.*

After that fiasco, I couldn't wait to see my *Fenn Street* friends again.

Contracted to do 14 out of 18 episodes, we began the second series of *Fenn Street* in October, but this time it was recorded at LWT's new studio, the

South Bank Television Centre, near the new National Theatre, the building of which had commenced in 1970 and it would be another four years until the opening. It was great to be in central London, and even greater to have Malcom returning as Peter Craven which made such a difference to the dynamic of each scene. I felt sorry for Léon Vitali, and often wondered how he must have felt, unless he concluded that his engagement had been, like a theatre understudy, a temporary measure. But I needn't have been concerned as in 1975, having played Lord Bullingdon in Stanley Kubrick's *Barry Lyndon*, he became the director's assistant, working on many of his films, including *The Shining*, in which he is credited as Assistant to the Director.

Prior to the first rehearsal for our new series, we spent a day filming the opening titles in Soho. Well, not filming exactly. A series of still photographs jerking rapidly like an old flicker book, which presumably circumvented any budgetary requirements for a filmed insert fee throughout the series. But at least, following the photoshoot in an amusement arcade in Wardour Street, a decent lunch with wine was provided at L'Escargot restaurant in Old Compton Street. This may have been on the insistence of Mark's new P.A., Myra, who if ever he looked like exploding, she always told him, 'Sweetness and light, Mark', and more often than not it seemed to work. Later, we discovered we had a new theme tune written by Denis King. And as every episode of the series was written by John and Bob, it looked like series two was going to be a huge improvement on the first series.

Richard Price was the Casting Director at LWT, who took over from Martin Case, the original casting director responsible for casting us regular 5C members and the *Please Sir!* staff. All of us 'gang' members often discussed the strange, and sometimes inept casting by Richard Price. Alastair Williamson as Mr Duffy was clearly Australian. Either Price knew of no actors capable of performing with an East End dialect, or he genuinely muddled Australian with Cockney. Hilda Fenemore was more comfortable in her role as Mrs Duffy as she was a native Londoner. But the casting that set our tongues wagging was in the first episode of series two *The Crunch*. Eric Duffy's older brother Monty had been built up in previous episodes of the first series as a lad to be reckoned with. Bit of a tough guy. Prentis Hancock was cast as Monty, and it became obvious he wasn't comfortable with the East End dialect, giving the impression that El's brother Monty was secretly educated at Eton and was masquerading as a cockney.

George Baker returned as Bowler for the next episode *Smart Lad Wanted*, a very funny episode. During a scene in a restaurant where Frankie devours

In *The Fenn Street Gang,* **George Baker plays the king of the district's underworld.** A scene from this week's show with **David Barry, right, and Malcolm McFee, centre**

an enormous gateau, after the recording Liz Gebhardt said with mock fury, 'All he does is eat a cake and he gets all the bloody laughs.' Some of the scenes with Bowler were hilarious. He now – much to Duffy's disapproval – employed Craven as a factotum and invited him to bring Frankie along 'as the little mad person... a sort of travelling cabaret.'

Sally Geeson was also in this episode as Bowler's daughter. Her second series of *Bless This House,* playing Sid James's daughter, was recorded between February and the end of May, and so she was free to appear in *Fenn Street.*

It was great to work with Barbara Mitchell again in episode three, *Menagerie á Trois,* where Frankie becomes jealous of her relationship with her lodger Cyril. The lodger was played by comedian Peter Glaze who for many years was in *Crackerjack.* Some of his scenes with Mrs Abbott were redolent of good old-fashioned mirth as he held her in a mock passionate embrace, raised a comedy leg behind him and shook it, suggesting to viewers that Crazy Gang humour often destroys reality on the small screen but can still be quite funny if you are easily pleased.

In this second series Barbara Keogh became well-established as Sharon's mum, and played her as much more of a floozy than had Diana Coupland. Also, there was more of a similarity between Carol's portrayal of Sharon and her mother.

I wasn't contracted to appear in the seventh episode of this series, and so I missed working with Mollie Sugden, although I appeared in an Asda commercial with her in the 1980s, playing her son-in-law. Many commercials are attended by the clients, and in this instance it was executives from Asda. These clients, often referred to as 'the suits', contrast sharply with the ad agency people who often dress casually or trendily, and the creative team hope the clients do not interfere too much in the shooting process. Tom Busman was director of this advert, and in a scene in which Mollie Sugden unloads her Asda shopping for her daughter and son-in-law, he said, 'This is the shot where Mollie unloads a cornucopia of tatty produce.' We laughed, but 'the suits' remained stony-faced.

Quite a few new characters made regular appearances in series two of *Fenn Street*. Apart from Barbara Mitchell and Peter Bayliss, Rosalind Elliot and Catherine Kessler appeared in many episodes. Rosalind played Celeste, and became Frankie's girlfriend by default, and Catherine played Rose who pairs up with Dennis. In the episode *Father's Day*, Eve Pearce, who played the downtrodden Mrs Dunstable in the *Please Sir!* film, revived the role for a scene in which she is bullied unmercifully by her odious husband but fights back, and Peter Bayliss gloried in a scene in which he became covered in all kinds of muck.

In this same episode, Dennis is taken by Rose to visit her parents, and her father was played by Bernard Kay, who was in the European tour of *Titus Andronicus*. He was surprised to find I was the same young man who played Young Lucius, Laurence Olivier's grandson in that production, as I had changed my name in the mid-sixties. He had one speech in *Titus Andronicus* as the Messenger, but we reminisced about that glittering 1957 tour to Paris, Venice, Belgrade, Zagreb, Vienna and Warsaw. In 1963, Bernard married Patricia Haines, Michael Caine's first wife.

Ruth Kettlewell played a dancing teacher in *The Loneliest Night of The Week*. It was great to meet up with her again, and I got her to share her BBC producer gaff with others in the cast. This episode was directed by Mark Stuart, and I had scenes with Madeline Mills playing a stripper who turns out to be a prostitute, and Abbott and she talk at cross purposes. Suddenly, in a scene break, Mark came down from the control room, and dragged me to the back of the set. 'For fuck's sake get her to pick up the pace. She's so fucking slow. She needs a rocket under her arse. For Christ's sake get her to put some fucking speed into it.'

I told Mark I'd try, but all I could really do was pick up my own cues quickly. I think Mark realized this and was clutching at straws.

But that's what Mark was like. He often moaned at us for waiting too long while the studio audience laughter died down. 'You are playing to the audience at home,' he would say. 'Not the studio audience. They are here for our benefit. Not the other way round.'

One of our floor managers was John West, but during camera rehearsals for one episode, while Mark and the vision mixer were in the control room, John said, thinking they couldn't hear him, 'One's daft and the other's deaf.' The curtain came down on his employment as floor manager for our series, just as it had with John Junkin. West was replaced by John Quilty who was an excellent floor manager, and quite diplomatic. When it came to conveying the director's instructions to Carol Hawkins, who has since told me that John Quilty was especially polite when he asked her to move more quickly to another position, without realizing she could hear Mark on John's headphones screaming, 'Tell that stupid fucking cow to move quicker over there.'

Another time one of the prop men showed me a butterfly bookmark which if you folded it and inserted it in the pages of a book, then opened it at that page, it would fly out. Feeling I needed to indulge in a childish prank, I borrowed the butterfly and a book, and in the middle of a camera rehearsal of a scene I wasn't in, a scene in which Carol sat at a dinner table, I crawled on my hands and knees unseen by the cameras, looked up at Carol and told her to open the book at a certain page. I hadn't expected quite such a startled reaction when the butterfly flew out. She jumped and screamed, while I crawled hastily away. And then I heard John Quilty explaining to the director that it was just an Abbott creature playing a silly joke. I think the director of this particular episode was Phil Casson who was always laid back. Had it been Mark Stuart in the control room I dread to think what an earful I would have got.

It's funny what some of us can and can't remember. When I mentioned this prank to Carol, she has no recollection of it at all.

Welsh actress Angharad Rees had recently played Gossamer Beynon in the *Under Milk Wood* film with Richard Burton and Elizabeth Taylor. In the *Fenn Street* episode *And Baby Makes Three,* she played a heavily pregnant young girl who is helped by Craven, who thinks she is soon to become a single mother. I loved working with her, and I avidly watched *Poldark* in the mid-seventies in which she played Demelza.

Is Anybody There? was an episode where we visit a spiritualist, Mr Grout, played by Donald Hewlett who played Colonel Reynolds in *It Ain't Half Hot Mum.* In this episode

Abbott goes into a park and tries to spook a toddler in a pushchair. The toddler, a child of no more than about 14-months-old, was wheeled in by her father, Geoffrey Davies, one of the regular cast members of the *Doctor* series, and his daughter Emma was given an ice cream cornet and was instructed to shove it into my face. But she wouldn't do it. This was going against what she had been taught she mustn't do. Instead, Philip Casson, director of this episode, making certain his hand was out of shot, took great delight in shoving it into my face.

In the penultimate episode of this series, Duffy, who has an office from which to run his painting and decorating business, advertises for a secretary. Madeleine Smith was an obvious choice to play the aptly-named Miss Bedwell, but her employment is short-lived, and Duffy engages Mrs Twinn, played by Lally Bowers, who was in the original West End production of *The Killing of Sister George*. We all got on very well with Lally, and I used to give her a lift home, because she lived not far from Liz and Ian's house, where I often stayed when we were doing the second series.

(Zélie and I had moved from Highgate Village and bought a house in Bedfordshire. It wasn't a good move and we relocated to Kingston-upon-Thames just over a year after our move to the country, prior to the start of the third series.)

Peter Cleall and I were in the queue one lunchtime in the LWT canteen, standing just behind Lally. Producer Verity Lambert, who was in the queue in front of Lally, happened to turn turned around and recognised her. 'Hello, Lally,' she said. 'What are you working on?'

'Fenn Street Gang,' Lally replied.

'Oh!' exclaimed the producer, as if Lally had told her she was appearing in a porn movie. And then Verity Lambert turned her back on Lally.

I don't know why Verity Lambert was so haughty about the *Fenn Street* series. After all, she would eventually produce the *El Dorado* soap, set in Spain. I watched two episodes. And the only reason I watched two was because I couldn't believe how bad the first one was and wanted to see if I'd imagined it.

I hadn't. It was terrible.

In the last episode of the series, *Absent Friends,* Duffy becomes engaged to Sharon, which was broadcast in February. Soon we were offered a third and final series, starting in less than three months' time. Liz was pregnant and had to turn it down, and Peter Denyer was also unavailable as he was signed up to do *No Sex Please We're British* for a summer season in Bournemouth. There would be eight episodes of the last series and us four remaining members of the cast were each contracted to appear in six out of eight episodes.

Commercial Break

Having been offered a commercial for Borzoi Vodka, I was sent the script. It made no bones about the character I was playing. It said so in the stage direction at the top of the page. Something like:

Frankie Abbott is in his cool bachelor pad entertaining three of the most ravishingly beautiful women who each represent a mix of vodka.

It was an unusually long advert, running to over three minutes, for showing in Scottish cinemas. I had a great deal of fast-paced dialogue in true Abbott-style, written by an ad agency copywriter who captured the character perfectly. I prepared myself for the lengthy rehearsal and, as is usual in most films, first would be a master shot, meaning the camera would take in the entire three minute scenario in a wide shot. The director watched through the viewfinder as I began to perform, putting some cool sounds on the stereo 'for you chicks'. When I got to the end of the scene, where I answer the telephone to my mother, saying I'd be home to tea right away, I noticed a huge grin on the director's face. Later he told me what he found so funny. As I began my Frankie Abbott routine, these three stunning top models couldn't quite believe what they were witnessing, and their mouths fell open like alarmed toddlers. This character was beyond their comprehension. Of course, they had never seen *Please Sir!* or *Fenn Street Gang* - they moved in different circles. Probably too busy swanning it in Anabel's or going on photo shoots with Lord Lichfield. It was brought home to me when during a break in the Green Room, I heard one of them stridently hurl across the room in a posh Chelsea voice, 'Yes, my dog plays with David Bailey's dog.'

And Then There Were Four

Rehearsals for the third series of eight episodes began in May and we were each contracted to appear in six episodes. It was odd performing without Peter Denyer and Liz, but now Barbara Mitchell and Rosalind Elliot's characters dominated some of the episodes, especially in the second episode *Mother Knows Best,* where Mrs Abbott becomes acutely jealous of Frankie's relationship with his new girlfriend and attempts to destroy it. John and Bob had already in a previous series given Abbott the middle name of Oedipus, now they took it a stage further and wrote a bizarre scene in which Frankie's mummy is bathing him. During the studio recording, a screen was put up masking the bathroom scene, and I jumped into the soapy bath – wearing a pair of swimming trunks, of course – prior to the start of the scene, so that it would get a huge laugh from the studio audience when the screen was whisked away to reveal Mrs Abbott using a loofah to scrub her little 'golden-haired elf.'

After capitalising on Mrs Abbott's jealousy of Celeste, in the third episode, *Alone at Last,* John and Bob presented us with another wedding as Duffy and Sharon get married, and the following episode *Making Whoopee* featured their honeymoon, which took place in Majorca (not really, not on LWT's budget).

Carol Hawkins has since told me that their Majorca exterior was an open-air swimming pool in Egham, set-decorated with palm trees. As it was by now winter, it was freezing cold, there was even snow on the ground. I must admit, when I saw this episode, which I wasn't in, they both convinced me they were enjoying their sun-baked swim, although Carol said at one stage Peter came up from under the water at the end of the take, crying 'Fucking hell!'

In episode five, *After the Ball,* we welcomed the return of Lally Bowers as Duffy's secretary. Duffy then employs a painter and decorator, Dwight D Rumbald, who turns out to be a lecher and keeps ogling Mrs Twinn until Duffy sends him packing. Mr Rumbald was played by Aubrey Morris, an actor who had appeared in dozens of films and television dramas including two cult films, *The Clockwork Orange* and *The Wicker Man*. His scenes with Lally Bowers were very funny, and the timing of both actors was superb.

The year before, Mark produced and directed *In For a Penny,* a situation comedy starring Bob Todd, Jack Woolgar and Ivor Salter, set in a public convenience. It ran for only six episodes and was abysmal. If we wanted to wind Mark up, we mentioned this series, and he always gritted his teeth before growling, 'Don't mention that show to me.'

We rehearsed for the final series of *Fenn Street* in a community centre just off Marylebone High Street. There was a trampoline up on the stage, and Mark, who directed five episodes of this final series, offered us lessons in trampolining. I became quite proficient at it, and I even had a go at a backward somersault once, although Mark tied a lunge around my waist as a safety harness. No way would he risk losing one of his leading actors in the middle of a series.

On day one of the read-through for the final episode, *Full Circle,* Bob Todd was playing yet another part, as an irate referee who falls out with Duffy and Craven during a football match, then dates Sharon's mother.

When Bob turned up on that first day, he opened his briefcase, took out a bottle of Scotch and asked Peter, Malcolm and me if we'd like a drink. It was ten in the morning and we stuck to coffee. But he poured himself a liberal measure in a cup. As the rehearsal progressed, and the pub opposite opened, he would dash across the road and come back with a gin or a vodka and tonic. Then he would forget where he had left these drinks which littered the rehearsal room. I was told he drank almost two bottles of spirits a day. It addled James Beck's memory, but not Bob Todd's. I met him about fifteen years later in the buffet on Tonbridge station. He had a glass in his hand, of course. He recognised me immediately. 'Hello, David,' he said affably. Which is quite a feat if you think about it. If it's true that he consumed two bottles of spirits a day, I worked it out that fifteen years' drinking at that level comes to 10,950 bottles.

When we began the recording in the studio for the final episode, though, there were a few tape breaks while Bob struggled to remember his lines. It was a dinner scene, and he placed his script on his dinner plate. John Quilty stopped the recording and told him it was a medium to wide shot and the television audience would see his script. Bob then put the script on the floor and bent over at an acute angle as he attempted to read the lines. But in the end, we managed to get through it.

And that was it. Following the recording, Mark booked a restaurant just off Baker Street which had a pianist, and we ended our six year stint with a singalong. Bob Larbey attended, but his long-time writing partner John Esmonde gave it a miss, and we all suspected he couldn't face the emotional parting after all the years we spent together.

Because we all knew this really was the end, it was an anti-climax, and I felt bereft for days afterwards. It was like departing from a family. But I soon recovered from any despondent feelings, because we had remained friends and would see one another again.

About three months after the series ended, I was asked to visit Mark at his office at LWT, to discuss writing another spin-off series about Duffy and Sharon buying a house in a rather upmarket housing estate. The idea was that Duffy's painting and decorating business had taken off, and their move to a more middle-class area meant that their posher neighbours tended to look down on them. But nothing ever came of this idea, as LWT decided it was a spin-off too many, especially considering the not entirely successful *Bowler* which was an Esmonde and Larbey spin-off from the *Fenn Street* series.

Because our series was still fresh in the public's mind, Bill Kenwright offered Peter Cleall, Malcolm McFee, Penny Spencer and me a tour of the Brian Rix farce *Dry Rot,* and we all agreed this would be fun to perform together. Our only concern was Penny's inaudibility on stage. We liked Penny very much but there was no way she could be heard in a large theatre, and no one used radio microphones in a play back then. But this concern was overshadowed by Kenwright's office telephoning our respective agents to say he couldn't get the rights to the John Chapman play and wanted us to do *Just Plain Murder* instead, a comedy thriller written by Roy Plomley, the creator and presenter of *Desert Island Discs,* who occasionally wrote mediocre plays few people would touch. We were all sent copies of his play and right away Peter turned it down, saying he wouldn't touch it with a bargepole. We were contacted directly by Kenwright who said he would give us permission to interfere with the play, change any lines or put in funny business. Peter wasn't tempted but Malcolm and I were.

Just Plain Murder was about three brothers plotting the death of their millionaire father's girlfriend when they discover she will inherit his money. Malcolm and I played two of the brothers, and Ian Masters was brought in to replace Peter. Despite the play's artistic shortcomings, it turned out to be a happy company.

Roy Plomley attended some of the early rehearsals. He wasn't too pleased with the way we chopped and changed things in the script but accepted it. He was only glad to get one of his plays into production.

After two weeks of trying to make this limpid play at least amusing, we travelled to Bath for a Sunday technical rehearsal. As soon as we walked on to the Theatre Royal stage, we were horrified to discover that the Kenwright organisation had cobbled together a makeshift set out of their scenery store, and the living room of our millionaire father looked more like an inner-city slum. The set was made up of two separate halves, one side of which was painted a ghastly magenta, and the other half was beige. The canvases on each flat were so loose they could have been used to sail across the Solent, and the paint was chipped and peeling. Everyone became depressed and the technical rehearsal was a complete waste of time. We drowned our sorrows in the Garrick's Head.

The following morning when we arrived at the theatre for the dress rehearsal, we found the resident theatre manager staring at the scenery as if in a deep coma. When he eventually came out of his trance, he dashed off to his office to phone Bill Kenwright, who agreed to catch the first train to Bath to sort something out. But we still had to open that night in front of a set that was a disgrace, and it was a tall order to expect the audience to suspend their disbelief beyond the blatant evidence of their eyes. Before them would be a constant reminder that the play must be located in a Glasgow tenement instead of a southern counties mansion.

We must have worked twice as hard to compensate for the scenery because the dress rehearsal went well. Bill arrived in time to see most of the play and he was complimentary about our performances.

While we had a break prior to the performance, he talked to the electrician's wife, who was a scenic designer and currently unemployed. During our break someone had bought an evening paper and discovered our set made headlines. The story told how our scenery was lost in transit from London and another set had to be borrowed for the show to open on time. The disaster turned from a negative into a positive, cast and management adopting a 'show must go on' spirit. We had no idea who gave this story to the press, but we realized it would help because the audience would know in advance what to expect as the curtain rose.

Despite the terrible scenery, the audience seemed to like the play, and it got quite a few laughs. One of the obstacles to overcome, though, was Penny's inaudibility. Any of her lines vital to the plot had to be repeated for the benefit of the audience.

(Penny: quietly) 'I'm just going to powder my nose.'

(One of us: loudly) 'Oh! You're just going to powder your nose?'

We managed to get through the show without any major disasters. As soon as the curtain came down, we all breathed a collective sigh of relief. Kenwright left a message apologising for not seeing the entire show as he had to dash back to London. In the Garrick's Head afterwards, the theatre electrician told us what happened during negotiations between the impresario and his wife, who had explained that magenta was a difficult colour to cover, needed maybe three coats of paint and would probably take three all night sessions to repaint the set. Kenwright asked for a price, and she told him it would cost eighty pounds. He paused before asking her, 'Would you paint half of it for forty?'

Every evening as we arrived at the theatre, we found a new oak beam running across a wall. The scenic designer went for a Tudor style. Bit by bit, over the next three days, our manor house took shape, so that by Friday we had a half decent set.

If only we had a half-decent play to perform. Which is why we started to muck about. Kenneth Shaw, an Australian actor, played a detective sergeant, and when he played a scene in which he called to question us three brothers, he wandered round the set nonchalantly picking up and examining various props. If he picked up a vase and looked underneath, a picture of a kangaroo would stare back at him. He managed to keep a poker face. It was Malcolm, Ian and me who spluttered with laughter and found it difficult to continue. The rot had set in. None of this was helped by Betty Alberge, who for more than four years played Florrie Lindley in *Coronation Street*. She gossiped in the wings and missed her entrances. Often, which was almost every night, our improvisation skills were put to the test. I actually found her late entrances became challenging and began to look forward to her missed entrances.

Another obstacle to overcome was working with Roy Hepworth, who often set us off giggling again. He was a slightly camp detective inspector, and wore too much make-up, as if plain clothes detectives never appear in public without blusher, lipstick and eye-shadow. Sometimes we couldn't look at each other when we were on stage with him, otherwise we would start corpsing.

Malcolm, Ian, Ken and I used to knock about together during the day, generally having a laugh and enjoying ourselves. The photo overleaf was taken in a pub garden just outside Bath, with left to right Malcolm McFee, Kenneth Shaw, me, Ian Masters and John Ingram (our Company Manager).

If only we didn't have to go into the theatre every night to perform that dreadful play, we all agreed. One day we made a resolution: we would get through the show without laughing. That night, as the curtain rose, I was determined not to corpse. I had the first speech in the play, talking to Ian,

plotting the murder of our father's mistress. As I was about to speak, I spotted a clown in a trench coat and trilby standing in the wings. Ken was wearing a clown's nose and this incongruous image had me snorting with laughter as I tried to deliver my opening lines. Ian, who had his back to the wings, was unaware of Ken's prank, and couldn't believe what was happening. Not five seconds into the play and he sees me corpsing. So much for a new-leaf resolution, he thought.

But there was worse to come. The following week in Bournemouth, our stage manager, Desmond Hoey, a southern Irishman who was fond of a drop, was responsible for the most ridiculous blunder. At the end of Act One, Penny's character, alone on stage, answers the telephone. The scene is set for her attempted murder. Dim lighting. Flickering firelight. As she picks up the phone, Penny acts out the realization that there is no one at the other end of the line as Desmond's Hoey's hand slides from behind a downstage door. We three suspects, the brothers, wait to make our entrance through the upstage door. Desmond's hand, holding a gun, is supposed to double for one of the suspects' hands. Penny turns on stage, a look of terror on her face as Desmond pulls the trigger. Click! Click! Nothing happens. The gun jams. Now anyone in their right mind should have stamped their foot or attempted some vocal simulation of a bang. Not our inventive and quick-thinking stage manager.

He throws the gun at her, and there is a dull thud as it lands on the rug at her feet. She attempts her usual, blood-curdling scream, which is our cue to enter. What we hear instead is a muffled giggle. Realizing something has gone wrong, we enter, to hear Penny's speech, which went something like this:

'I was wanted on the phone. But there was no one on the other end of the line. The lights were out. And then, in the flickering shadows of the fire, I saw a hand come from behind that door. And then someone… threw a gun at me.'

After that, we found it difficult to continue. Fortunately, there was an explosive special effect which closed the act, some nonsense about a television set blowing up.

During the day, the four of us continued to enjoy ourselves, occasionally meeting up with Penny or Betty for lunch or afternoon tea. Then, towards the end of the week, our company was invited to take tea at a vicarage. Every touring company performing in Bournemouth was invited to visit Mrs Yorke-Battley. Widowed years ago, her husband had been the theatre chaplain and made an allowance in his will for money to be set aside to entertain performers at least once during their visit to the town.

On the vicarage lawn we played croquet, had photographs taken by David, the young curate, and thumbed through mounds of heavy photograph albums showing pictures of all the theatre companies who had visited Mrs Yorke-Battley. Then we were invited inside for tea, consisting of boiled eggs, bread and butter, scones and tea cakes, and either tea or sherry. We all chose the sherry, served in miniscule glasses. Two sips later, the sherry downed, Mrs Yorke-Battley asked, 'Hands up who would like some more sherry?' I've never seen hands raised so fast.

After tea, we were invited to play a game of whist, and the person trumped had to shout out daringly, 'Oh, hell!'

The visit to the vicarage was a wonderful time-warp experience. None of us would have been surprised to find George Bernard Shaw in plus-fours playing croquet on the sumptuous lawn. The only reminder of the more permissive, swinging times was Penny's disappearance to the loo to roll a joint.

If I said there was worse to come about the gun incident, I take it back. The pistol hurling paled into insignificance with the next episode of theatrical embarrassment – again engineered by our stage manager. After Bath and Bournemouth, the Corby Civic Theatre was strictly fourth division. So, performing to a house of mainly senior citizens during the midweek matinee, we didn't expect there to be anyone in the audience who was a card-carrying member of Equity, let alone someone as esteemed as a Royal Shakespeare Company player who happened to be in the area.

Prior to the matinee, Desmond had a lunchtime drink in a nearby pub where he met one of the locals with a Pyrenean Mountain Dog, an animal that is built like a small pony. By now, flushed after several drinks, our stage manager persuaded the dog's owner to let him borrow it for ten minutes. While the show was up and running, Desmond sneaked back to the pub and returned minutes later with the enormous hound. Giggling at his devilish plan to have some fun and games, he talked Ken Shaw into taking the dog on stage as his police dog.

I wasn't in that particular scene and I watched the events from the wings. Ian and Malcolm gave Ken the cue to enter. The set door opened and in strolled the humongous hound, dragging behind him a bemused detective sergeant, who was straining to hold back this friendly but awe-inspiring mutt. Once over their initial shock, Ian and Malcolm had difficulty getting their lines out as they attempted to suppress their giggles, especially as they watched Ken's predicament as he struggled to restrain this dog who had the strength of an ox. Eventually, realizing the scene was collapsing, they managed to recover slightly, and in between snorts managed to keep to the script and get out some essential plot lines. Until the dog, which stood chest high to Malcolm and Ian, suddenly lowered his mighty head to sniff Ian's balls. That finished all three actors who were now helpless with laughter. And the dog, weary of this unprofessional behaviour, turned and exited through the open door, dragging the detective after him.

Ian and Malcolm were left on stage with still another half page of scene to perform with Ken. But he was gone and had slammed the door behind him. They struggled for a while, and cut most of the scene, leaving out some plot developments.

As we sat in the communal male dressing room after the show, there was a forceful knock on the door. Before anyone had a chance to invite someone to enter, the door was flung open and in walked a man, accompanied by his partner. He was clearly angry. We all wondered who this could be. Ian, catching the man's eye in the mirror, swivelled in his chair and greeted him, rather sheepishly I noticed. It was an actor Ian knew, an actor from the Royal Shakespeare Company. He told us what he thought of the show in no uncertain terms.

'It has to be the worst performance I have ever had the misfortune to sit through,' he barked. 'There is no excuse for that sort of behaviour. There may not have been many people in the audience, but they still paid to sit through that unprofessional behaviour.'

Ian stammered and tried to make excuses. The actor waved excuses aside and ranted and raved about how disgustingly unprofessional we all were, and his partner shook her head and tutted disapproval.

Suddenly, the actor rounded on Roy Hepworth. 'As for you,' he said, pointing at Roy's face, 'you're a clown. I've never seen such ridiculous make-up on a policeman before.'

Once the actor and his partner departed, a deathly silence fell on the dressing room. We were all humbled by what was clearly the truth. But Roy, having recovered from the initial shock of being described as a 'clown', began blustering about the man's cheek, saying, 'Who does he think he is, barging into our dressing room like that.'

Ian was full of abject apologies and was deeply embarrassed. But when the four of us were safely ensconced in the flat we rented, as we reminisced about the day's events we were soon in stitches again.

At Horsham Capitol Theatre, for our final week of the tour, there was one other episode which ranked highly in theatrical bad behaviour, and whilst not in the gold medal standard of the dog incident, it came a close second with silver. Again, our fond-of-a-drop stage manager featured greatly in the incident.

One night something happened which set us off again and we were almost helpless with laughter. We almost succeeded in controlling ourselves, had it not been for Desmond who decided to admonish us while we were still performing. His florid face appeared in the set's fireplace. If any of the audience saw it, glowing amongst the embers, they must have thought the play had taken a surrealistic turn. Then the florid face spoke.

'Come on!' it urged. 'Pull yourselves together, you bastards!'

That finished us completely. Our last week ended in a blaze of shameful behaviour.

Looking back on it, I think it was probably the worst time of my career. I have always prided myself on behaving as a consummate professional, but the actor who burst into our dressing room in Corby was right. We behaved disgracefully, and it was unfair on audiences who paid good money to see the play.

But faced with this dichotomy, bad behaviour versus professionalism, if I'm really honest I have to admit I've never had so many laughs as I did on that tour.

Later in the year I was offered my first pantomime, *Cinderella* at the Granada East Ham, a venue which had a history of live events performed in this vast, almost two-thousand seat cinema. The management was none other than Bill Kenwright, and Buttons was played by Tony Blackburn with Anne Aston from *The Golden* Shot in the title role.

I played Frankie, one of the Broker's Men, and the other half of this double act was played by Monty Wells, with whom I got on extremely well, and we got together to rehearse privately, using bowler hat routines for our opening scene.

Anna Karen played Fairy Godmother, and on the first day of rehearsal she grabbed me by the hand, took me aside, and told me Roy Hudd had taught her a comedy balloon dance, which we did as a speciality act in the ballroom scene, dressed as ballet dancers with a balloon sandwiched between us. This worked brilliantly until the New Year's Eve show when Anna had had a few drinks and the balloon went everywhere except where it was supposed to go.

The director of this show was more at home giving orders to boy scouts. It became apparent early on in rehearsals that Ralph Reader couldn't cope with directing us, although he had written, choreographed and directed the *Gang Show* for decades. He was another casualty of the demon drink. Pissed for most of the rehearsals, he occasionally snoozed at his director's table, woke up suddenly, told us we were rubbish and asked us to do it again. During one disastrous rehearsal, Monty and I were rehearsing the Sondheim number 'Wherever We Go' with the Ugly Sisters, played by Terri Gardner and Hugh Futcher, and we were being choreographed by Reader. Having trouble following his steps as he was particularly inebriated on this occasion, Hugh Futcher had had enough, and said, 'I'm not doing that. It's poxy!' Reader, glassy-eyed, stared at him, waved the objection aside and said, 'Oh well, do it yourself then.'

Despite this non-direction, the cast managed to get the show up to a reasonable standard, and we were full almost every night with block bookings taken from many organisations such as Ford Cars at Dagenham, who had a major workforce then. But the person I most enjoyed working with was Valentine Dyall as Baron Hard-up. Val had a very dry sense of humour, a glass-eye, which gave him a rather sinister aspect, and a wonderful voice, which he used for many years in the 1950s and '60s when he was the voice of 'The Man in Black', horror and ghost stories on BBC Radio.

As I lived in Kingston-upon-Thames, every night after the show I gave Val a lift to Waterloo station where he caught his train home. I remember him telling me he was a keen golfer, and he had been declared bankrupt. He was deeply concerned because he belonged to Sunningdale Golf Club and was worried how their committee might respond to his unfortunate predicament. Then a request came for him to appear before the club secretary and several committee members. With a despondent heart he went along to be told that they liked having him as a member, had heard about his problems, therefore they agreed he should be made an honorary member. Val said he was so overcome by their kindness and understanding, he burst into tears.

Early in the spring of 1974 we got our first colour television set, and it didn't cost me a bean. I was offered a photo shoot for three advertisements in Sunday newspaper colour supplements, advertising National Panasonic. For the hour-long shoot I was paid five-hundred pounds plus a gift of five-hundred pounds' worth of their equipment. Colour televisions were still quite expensive then, but there was still enough left over for stereo equipment and a radio alarm. These gadgets arrived one morning by black cab and we tore open the packaging excitedly then watched our first programme in colour.

Prior to the pantomime, I co-wrote with Ian Talbot a sketch show, *The Lads from Fenn Street*. We talked about this during the last series of *Fenn Street,* and as we needed permission to use the television characters, we approached John and Bob, who happily gave their consent. Malcolm contacted Peter Denyer, who was doing his summer season in Bournemouth, but he wasn't interested in either performing or directing it. We asked Christopher Timothy to direct and he agreed, adding some great ideas and sketches to the script. At that time, Chris was contracted to do hard-sell television commercials for the *Sun* newspaper, and he wrote one of the sketches, a spoof of himself, with Malcolm playing him.

During a break in the rehearsals, Chris told us a very funny story about when he worked with Laurence Olivier at the Old Vic, playing his page in *Othello*. Prior to exiting, Olivier threw Chris a handful of coins for which he scrambled about, picking them up off the stage, and popping them into his pouch. While this was going on, Olivier gave his final mighty speech and exited to a round of applause. The next day, while Chris was in his office, he suggested it might be neater and cleaner if Olivier threw him just one coin.

'All right, baby,' Olivier replied. 'We will try that tonight.'

Chris came away thinking he had just been cheeky enough to give the great actor direction. But when it came to the evening performance, Olivier, having taken the suggestion on board, threw Chris a single coin. Unfortunately, Chris made an extravagant gesture to catch it, missed, and the coin rolled towards the edge of the stage and the front row. To save face, Chris stamped on it, tossed it in the air, and caught it nimbly in his pouch, where it dropped neatly to the bottom. The audience, appreciating this elaborate bit of business, applauded heartily. Oliver gave his speech and exited. No applause.

Now that he had ruined Othello's exit, Chris was slightly scared of bumping into him again. Then, as he walked along a corridor backstage, he saw Olivier coming towards him. As he drew level, without looking at Chris, but with a twinkle in his eye, he passed by and muttered one word: 'Cunt!'

When Chris told us the story we fell about, appreciating Olivier's humour, who pretended to react as if the young actor had deliberately set out to upstage him.

As Malcolm, Peter and I met for the first time at Stonebridge Park we decided to call our production company Stonebridge Productions. First, we played some small halls in the suburbs of London to try our show out initially before taking it on an 18 week tour, a tour which varied from one and two night-stands to a week in some of the larger theatres, such as Swansea Grand Theatre.

This became one of my favourite venues, run by John Chilvers, who watched our show several times, and told us his favourite sketch was the *Crossroads* spoof with Malcolm as Meg Richardson and me as Amy Turtle. When I mentioned working in Roy Plomley's *Just Plain Murder,* he told me the radio presenter kept submitting terrible plays to him which he always turned down.

One of the notable features backstage at the Grand, which has disappeared since the theatre was revamped, was a ladder halfway up the stairs leading to the dressing rooms. At the top of the ladder was a hatch, and if you knocked on this door it would slide open to reveal a barmaid's ankles. The hatch was on the floor behind the counter in the dress circle bar and it enabled performers or stage crew to purchase a drink, but only during the running of the show when the audience was seated in the auditorium, never during the interval. It would be disconcerting for a member of the audience to see an actor's face peering from a hole at shoe level like a wee timorous beastie.

We three were never able to make use of the hatch as we rarely left the stage, except for quick costume changes.

Another feature of this theatre was Sir Henry Irving's signature on his baggage label, encased in glass on the door of the number one dressing room. John Chilvers told us about a touring rock 'n' roll show visiting the

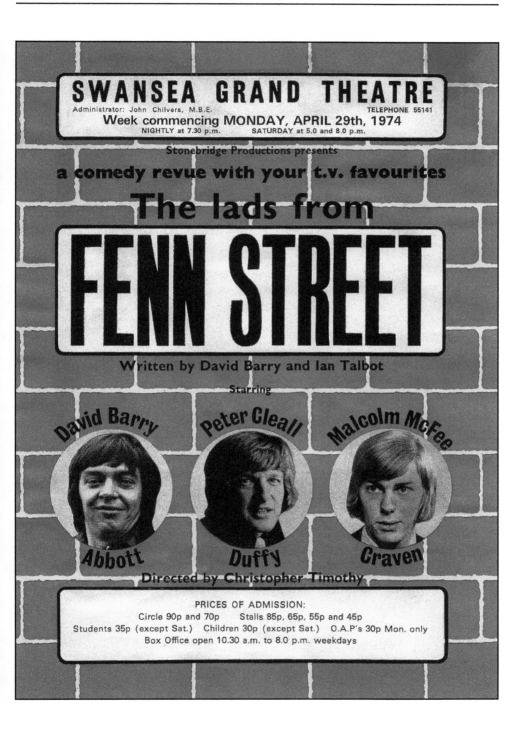

theatre. He showed the lead singer around backstage and explained about the legendary actor's signature. 'This is Sir Henry Irving's signature,' he said. 'The Grand Theatre Swansea was his penultimate performance. After that he went up north, where he died.'

'Well,' replied the rock singer, 'don't they all in those northern clubs?'

During the week in Swansea I had to catch an early train back to London for a half day's filming – a religious film made by Churches Television and Radio Centre. The film was called *Support Your Local Poet* and I performed a voice-over poem while sitting opposite Caroline Munro at a candlelit dinner. Caroline was hugely familiar from the Lamb's Navy Rum campaign and also became a Bond girl as Naomi in *The Spy Who Loved Me*. As I sat opposite her, playing a rather smooth young man who wondered where this dinner would lead, my voice-over suddenly revealed to me a spiritual truth that I was being rather shallow, and I suddenly saw the light and was saved. And if you believe that…

When I got back to Swansea in time for the show that evening, Peter and Malcolm were in the hotel room having an early supper bought at a fish and chippie. They complained that their portion of chips and scallops was a double portion of potatoes, little realizing that scallops in Welsh fish and chip shops are potatoes dipped in batter. I asked them how much the scallops cost, and when they told me, I said, 'Well, the price should have given you a clue you weren't getting seafood scallops!'

Having a drink in a Swansea pub we met a Welshman who hated the actor Kenneth Haigh, and thought the man was a pig. I wanted to know why because, although I had never worked with the actor, whenever I drank in Gerry's club, I always talked to Kenneth Haigh, and he seemed very pleasant. But in Gerry's there was an unwritten rule, you never pestered anyone for autographs, which is why it was a club where actors could escape from all that. And it transpired that this Welshman on a trip to London was taken by an acquaintance to Gerry's Club one night, and as he had seen Kenneth Haigh in *Man At The Top*, he went over to him, handed him a sheet of paper and asked if he wouldn't mind putting his moniker on that.

'And he just told me to fuck off!' said the outraged Welshman.

When Malcolm and I first began booking dates for this tour, we hoped to get a few reasonably close to London so that we could invite a few television producers along to see it; but the nearest venue we managed to book was at East Grinstead. We invited Michael Grade, who was Head of Light Entertainment at LWT, never thinking he would accept our invitation, so we were surprised and pleased when he made the journey one rainy midweek night, and we picked him up at the railway station. We had a drink with him after the show, which he said he enjoyed, but no offers of sketch shows were ever forthcoming from LWT after that.

We discovered the greatest difficulty in booking tours is in trying to get them within reasonable travelling distance of each other. I think the longest journey we had to make was from a few one-night stands in the Cheshire area to Kirkcaldy in Fife. At least we could relax at the Adam Smith Centre because we were booked for the entire week on a guarantee, and the bookings were reasonably good. We stayed at the Station Hotel, conveniently close to the theatre, and on Friday night after the show we were in the bar when the hotel manager said there was an event going on in their function room and people would love to meet us. We joined the event, which looked as if it might have been some sort of dinner and dance which started much earlier in the evening. Thinking we might plug our show for the last two Saturday performances, we got up on the stage and performed a couple of short sketches, and I sang a short song from the show.

Sweet Fanny Adams,
Always bright and gay.
In the old apple tree in the orchard
We carved our names one day.
But the woodpecker came in September
And woodpecker wood peck away,
Now all we can see on the old apple tree
Is sweet F.A!

Then Malcom said something like, 'I hope you are all having a good evening, and are a bit pissed like we are, and please come and see our last two performances at the Adam Smith Centre.'

The organiser of this event, a dour looking giant in a kilt, came over and said, 'I'd like you to leave now.'

We laughed. This guy had a real dry sense of humour, and because we'd entertained them at his function free of charge, we waited for him to say something like, 'What'll you have to drink, lads?' Then we realized by his sour expression that he was deadly serious. What had upset him we wondered? Was it my sweet F.A. line? Or was it Malcolm using the word pissed. Whatever it was, his attitude was extreme. When several woman asked us for autographs, we apologised, saying we had to leave as their organiser was throwing us out.

We never found out what his problem was, unless he was some nutty Bible-thumping bigot who hated *The Fenn Street Gang*. But at least our theatre performances went down well at the Adam Smith Centre.

In 1974, like Wales, the pubs shut on Sundays in Scotland, so on the Sunday morning as we drove to our next venue and crossed the border, we stopped for a lunchtime drink at the first pub in England. We had just got our drinks when someone said, 'How's your tour going?'

The chap introduced himself. He recognised us because he was an actor touring in another show, on their way from Bournemouth to Aberdeen, and decided to stop off for a final drink before the last leg of their marathon journey.

We arrived at the Key Theatre, Peterborough just as Sir Harmer Nicholls, Conservative M.P. for Peterborough was leaving, having been shown around the theatre. We were introduced to him, and it was much later I discovered he was the father of Sue Nicholls, the actress with whom I had worked in *Crossroads* in the mid-sixties.

Later Peter reminded us that in the 1966 general election, there were seven recounts in Peterborough as Sir Harmer Nicholls won by only three votes, which has to be the closest result ever.

It was in Peterborough I seem to remember coming down to breakfast in the hotel we stayed at, and one of the chambermaids spotted us and said, 'Fenn Street Gang! I recognised you. You look just like yourselves.'

Ken Shaw, who played the detective sergeant in *Just Plain Murder*, we employed to market the show, which is how I ended up fighting two rounds wrestling Albert 'Rocky' Wall. We'd been playing a few one-night stands up north, and we had a Saturday free. Our next venue was the Pier Pavilion Cleethorpes, so we decided to drive over there, book into a hotel, then have a look at the venue. When we arrived at the theatre, a band was getting their equipment into a large vehicle. We asked them what the venue was like, and they gave us their eye-rolling verdict of terrible, having played to only a dozen people. We asked the name of their group and were told it was Showaddywaddy, soon to reach number two in the charts with 'Hey Rock and Roll'.

Our publicity stunt took place on the Sunday night when I climbed into the boxing ring to challenge 'Rocky' Wall. I wore a great cape, Bermuda shorts and boxing gloves. Peter and Malcolm, as my seconds wore snazzy sequined jackets and bowler hats. I pranced around the ring, waving gloved fists in the air, saying 'I am the greatest.' It was then I got a bit worried because 'Rocky' looked towards his manager as if to say, 'Why didn't you tell me about this stunt?' Then he grabbed me, raised me above his head, and slammed me on to the canvas. But he knew exactly what he was doing, and I didn't feel a thing. He grunted and shouted, squeezing me in a neck lock as I struggled to think what happens next. 'Submit, you idiot!' Malcolm and Peter shouted. After I'd capitulated, we fought another round, I submitted again, and the champion wrestler retained his title. Not that he was ever in any danger from Frankie in his Bermuda shorts. Afterwards, he fought his proper round and beat his opponent. Following the match, we met both the wrestlers and their wives for a pint in the nearest bar. Later, I admitted 'Rocky' was an excellent actor who had me worried for a moment. But it was worth it because we made the front pages of the newspapers on Monday.

Our show was also booked for a week at Hull Arts Centre, a small theatre which later became the base for Hull Truck Company. Advance bookings were poor, and Ken arranged for us to make a brief appearance at a cabaret club, where the resident DJ would plug our show prior to Gerry and the Pacemakers performing. We stayed to watch the show, and Gerry Marsden not only sang all his popular hits, but invited some members of the audience to participate in 'Old MacDonald Had a Farm', which worked well, as many of the participants were uninhibited through alcohol, and prepared to be the butt of Gerry's jokes.

The singer heard that some of the *Please Sir!* cast were visiting and invited us to join him in his dressing room after the show for a few drinks. As Gerry's cabaret performance wasn't until quite late, we invited him to see our show on Tuesday night. He came and liked the show so much, he returned to see the midweek matinee, bringing his wife and family. Then he invited us to have a drink with him after his performance on Friday night.

We arrived a bit early and he was still on stage. But he had left word to expect us and we were shown into his dressing room and told to help ourselves to the Scotch he had left out.

Suddenly his manager or roadie barged in, behaving as if he owned the place. He began criticising Gerry's act and we thought this must be Mister Ten Per Cent. Definitely his agent, the way he spoke about his client. When Gerry arrived, he gave the man a cursory nod. Then the bloke launched into a criticism of his act, going on and on in running down Gerry's performance. Suddenly, the singer could take it no more, pointed his finger at the man and demanded, 'What do you do, pal?'

'I'm a gas fitter.'

Gerry exploded. 'You're a gas fitter and you're telling me how to do my act. Go on, clear out!'

The man exited hurriedly, and Gerry turned to us and apologised. 'I'm sorry, lads, if he was a colleague of yours. But I couldn't take all that shit after a show.'

We said we'd never seen him before. 'The way he spoke we thought he must have been your agent,' Malcolm said.

Gerry laughed. 'Good job I thought he was with you lads, else I might have chinned him.'

The photo below shows the 'Lads' outside the White Rock Pavilion, Hastings, performing from Monday to Saturday. And dig those crazy flares, man!

Our show did well in the south, and in Scotland and Wales, but not so well in the north of England. I often used to wonder if this was because of some myth about northerners not liking southerners. One small venue in the north, and I really can't remember where it was, we played for two nights. Prior to our tour they demanded a great deal of publicity material.

When we arrived at the venue I could see in the box office a huge pile of our posters lying around. It put me in a terrible mood, angry not so much about the cost of the posters but the fact that they hadn't been used to publicise the show. I demanded to see the manager who was not available until the interval. After the first half the manager came into the dressing room and I launched into a tirade about how badly run the theatre was. I expected Malcolm at least to back me up, but he snuck out of the dressing room, stifling a smile. I was astounded. When he returned I asked him why he hadn't stayed to back me up. And he told me he found it difficult to keep a straight face.

'How can anyone take you seriously, ranting and raving, when you're dressed as Little Bo-Peep?'

Another northern date we played was in Preston, Lancashire. The first night at the hotel I hardly got any sleep as my room backed onto the railway lines, and diesels hummed and throbbed all night long. Unable to sleep, I telephoned reception and asked, 'What time does this hotel arrive at Euston?'

The three of us moved to a quieter hotel in Lytham St. Anne's for the rest of the week.

Because the curtain didn't come down on our show until the pubs almost called last orders, we went to nightclubs for drinks, and occasionally a late meal. We were often pestered for autographs if we were recognised, which we didn't mind. Except when we were eating, and our meal was interrupted by an insensitive person demanding an immediate signature. But the biggest intrusion came when we were at Torquay and Peter went into a public convenience. When he came out, nonplussed and shaken, he told us he'd been standing at the urinal enjoying a pee when a man standing at the next stall recognised him and demanded an autograph.

And that's what *The Lads from Fenn Street* was like. We had loads of laughs, even though we made little money. Our takings had been used up on meals, drinks and hotels. We lived well but had little to show for it by the end of the tour. Peter was offered some television work and resigned from Stonebridge Productions, leaving Malcolm and me to plan our next project – a large-scale tour of *Under Milk Wood*.

Commercial Break

I was cast as a leather-jacketed yob - surprise, surprise! - in a television commercial for a bottled beer - McEwen's Export, I think - for showing in Northern Ireland. The ad was shot in an Irish pub in Whitechapel Road, on the corner of Cambridge Heath, opposite the Blind Beggar on the other corner, which was the pub notorious for the Ronnie Kray murder of George Cornell in 1966.

I and another actor drank beer from early in the morning, and the drinking lasted as long as the shoot, which was all day. The message of this ad was a simple one. You might be a loser it implied, but drink our beer and you'll be a winner, because as we leant on the bar sipping the brew, the door opened and in came Joanna Lumley, looking radiant in a diaphanous dress, and naturally the Greek goddess was attracted to these two yobs.

It was a simple minded ad for simple minded people.

There was a small location catering wagon outside the pub, where I spotted the chef with a fag in his mouth, ash dropping into the food. I got on well with the cinematographer and when we broke for lunch we decided ash-free pub grub in the Blind Beggar was preferable to the chuck wagon. We crossed the street and entered the pub. As we walked up to the bar, the young barmaid recognised me and got quite excited. 'Frankie! What are you doing here?' she said, smiling. Without hesitating I dropped into character. 'I heard there was a spot of bother in here,' I replied, 'So I thought I'd come down and sort it out.'

The pub went quiet, the smile left the barmaid's face and she excused herself to serve another customer further along the bar.

Perhaps a gin and tonic in the Blind Beggar was a bad idea on top of all the strong beer I'd drunk, because by late afternoon I was feeling very pissed, and the final shot of the day was a dirty great close-up of me seeing Joanna Lumley's entrance into the pub. My reaction now would have been over the top viewed from the upper circle at Drury Lane. John Crome, the director, asked me if I could give a smaller reaction. My next reaction was numbed inscrutability. 'You didn't do anything that time,' he said. Eventually, he kept the camera rolling and I gave many different reactions, some big, some small. After this mixed-bag of reactions he got what he wanted, because it was a wrap and they poured me into a car and gave the driver my address.

But I had other ideas. Instead of heading for Kingston-upon-Thames I redirected the driver to Gerry's Club. I can't recall what happened after that...

Bernard Hedges meets the notorious 5C, Series 1, 1968

A Fenn Street Gang and 5C publicity still

please sir!

goedhartige
barbaren

A Dutch novelisation of episodes from the first series

Please Sir! staff and 5C pose for Look-In Magazine

Sixty of the cast and crew it took to record one episode

5C bunk off school in episode 1 of Series 3

Nobbler with 5C in their trashed camp hut

The official school photograph of 5C and staff members

In the film, Frankie is tucked up safely with his 'mascot'

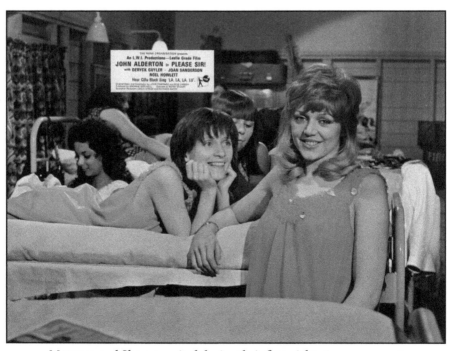

Maureen and Sharon excited during their first night at summer camp

'Strong him, El! Strong him!'

Norman Potter inadvertently lets slip that it was he who forged Mr Dunstable's signature

Posed publicity still for the film

Another posed shot

The Fenn Street Gang series goes into Look-In

The Lads from Fenn Street at their true home

The Fenn Street alumni at an LWT reunion

The 'lads' tangle with wrestler Albert 'Rocky' Wall

Husband and Wife in Cloud Nine, Nightingale Theatre, Brighton

Please Sir!

WHERE DID EVERYONE GO?

ITV, Sunday
Forever Green

The classroom chaos of *Please Sir!* made it one of the top comedies of the late Sixties and early Seventies. The ITV programme starred John Alderton as schoolteacher Bernard Hedges, in charge of the worst class at the tough Fenn Street Secondary Modern School.

You can see John as Jack Boult in the current series of *Forever Green*. And in a few weeks there is the chance to see again the pilot episode of *Please Sir!*, when it is included in C4's *TV Heaven*. But where are all those Fenn Street faces now? Steve Clark tracked them down.

Maureen Bullock
Liz Gebhardt

Goody, goody Maureen Bullock was played by Liz Gebhardt who loved every minute. 'Someone once described Maureen as the shiny penny in a muddy stream,' says Liz. Since *Please Sir!* and its successor *The Fenn Street Gang*, Liz, now 46, has worked extensively in the theatre and on television, including, *Bulman*, *Grange Hill* and *Brookside*.

She lives in south London with her actor/director husband Ian Talbot and 18-year-old son Joe.

In a class of their own — when it came to causing chaos and confusion — were, from left to right above: Maureen Bullock (Liz Gebhardt), Frankie Abbott (David Barry), Eric Duffy (Peter Cleall), Peter Craven (Malcolm McFee) and Dennis Dunstable (Peter Denyer). The teacher with the tough task of trying to keep them in check was Bernard Hedges (John Alderton), here with the adoring Sharon Eversleigh (Penny Spencer)

Frankie Abbott
David Barry

Daft Frankie Abbott lived in a fantasy world of comics. Played by David Barry, he was the coward who saw himself as a tough guy. David has subsequently been in *Brookside* and at Christmas was in pantomime with Gorden Kaye at Aldershot in a production that was written by his *Please Sir!* colleague Peter Denyer.

David, 48, who also wrote several episodes of the comedy series *Keep It In the Family*, lives in Kent with his actress wife Pat Carlile, daughter Emma, nine, and son Morgan, six.

Eric Duffy
Peter Cleall

He was a big hit in the role of rough-diamond troublemaker Duffy — but at the time Peter Cleall was already a married man . . . and he is a former public schoolboy. Recently he appeared in *EastEnders* as a boat owner named Malcolm who shopped Clyde to the police, and later this year Peter will be seen in a new BBC TV series *Growing Pains*.

He is married to his second wife, actress Dione Inman. They have two sons, Dan, four, and two-year-old Spencer.

Peter Craven
Malcolm McFee

While in *Please Sir!*, Malcolm McFee hit the headlines by marrying a real-life teacher. Says Malcolm: 'I met my wife, Maggie, at a party and she came to see one of the recordings — I think she thought I was a cameraman. She was astonished when she saw me playing a pupil!' Since then he has been in many TV shows, worked in the theatre, and is also an advertising copywriter. He and Maggie live in east London with their 11-year-old daughter Victoria.

Dennis Dunstable
Peter Denyer

The part of dozy Dennis Dunstable suited Peter Denyer: 'They told me I got the job because I looked more stupid than anyone else who was auditioned!' he says with a rueful smile.

Bachelor Peter, 44, who is also remembered as boring Ralph Dring in the BBC comedy *Dear John*, now spends most of his time writing, directing and producing shows, mainly pantomimes, from an office in his Victorian house in Gloucestershire.

'It's ridiculous,' he says, 'a lot of people run away from offices to be actors — I've run away from being an actor to work in an office!'

Bernard Hedges
John Alderton

Gullible Bernard Hedges — who had the misfortune to be employed to teach Fenn Street's rough, tough Form 5C — made John Alderton a household name. John, 51, went on to appear in numerous TV and stage productions, including *Upstairs Downstairs* and *Thomas and Sarah*, both of which also starred his wife Pauline Collins, who now stars with him in *Forever Green*.

John and Pauline live in north London with their children Nicholas, Catherine and Richard.

Sharon Eversleigh
Penny Spencer

Form 5C's mini-skirted temptress Sharon Eversleigh, was played by Penny Spencer who left the series in 1971 saying: 'People were calling me Penny and thinking I was Sharon, or vice versa. I began to wonder who I was!'

Penny, 45, and her second husband Ross Carver had their first child, Kate, in 1975 and Penny has subsequently taken time off from acting.

Carol Hawkins, now 43, took over the part of Sharon and has since worked extensively in theatre and on TV. Her husband Martyn Padbury is a clairvoyant and healer.

In 1979 the TV Times wondered what had happened to us

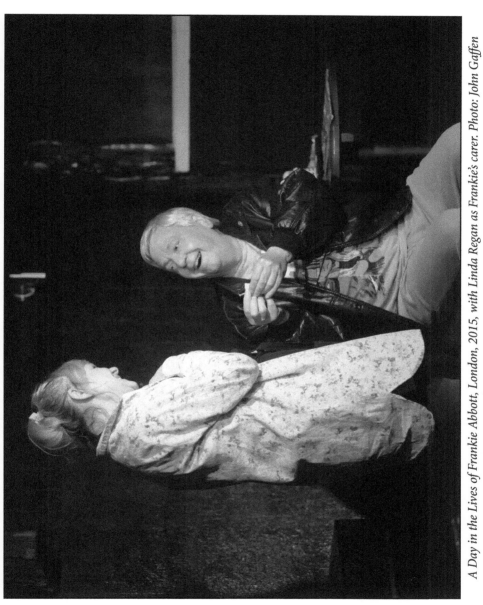

A Day in the Lives of Frankie Abbott, London, 2015, with Linda Regan as Frankie's carer. Photo: John Gaffen

On The Road Again

Our house in Kingston wasn't far from Barbara Mitchell's home, where she lived with her family. Recently, Zélie told me that when we first moved in, Barbara came round with a greetings card and a cup of sugar as a welcome to the neighbourhood, but I don't remember that. But I do remember seeing her on many occasions at the local shops, and she would always shout across the street, 'Just come out to buy some chips, Frankie?'

We were both invited as guests on *The Golden Shot*, which was televised from their ATV studios in Birmingham. Bob Monkhouse made us most welcome, and said he loved our characters. Monkhouse was amused when I told him that my first ever TV show in 1955 was his show broadcast live from Shepherd's Bush Empire, in which he attempted to make me laugh with a string of gags while I stared at him expressionlessly, until he went down on one knee for his tagline, hoping I would eventually crack my face. Instead, I brought an egg from behind my back and cracked that on his head.

It was great travelling to Birmingham with Barbara when I could spend some time chatting to her. She also involved me in appearing for many local charities around Kingston, joining her and her husband Rex. Barbara did some great work following *Fenn Street,* when she appeared in *Beryl's Lot* and played Irene Handel's daughter in *For The Love of Ada.* It was a great shock when she suddenly died in 1977 from cancer at the age of 48, as no one knew she was ill. Apparently, or so I heard later, not many people knew she was dying, as she wanted it kept quiet, so that she could continue working as near to the end as possible.

But it is as my mother that I will always remember her, especially in the *Please Sir!* film when she delivers that fantastic line, 'Don't do that, my duck, you know Dickie don't like it', as I squirt the budgerigar with washing-up liquid. What a great person and a great comic actress. The perfect foil for a character like Frankie Abbott.

That same year I heard the news that Erik Chitty had died, just a few months before Barbara Mitchell. He was only seventy-years-old, five years younger than Noel Howlett, but because of the parts he played he always seemed older than he was. When he played Smithy starting in the summer of 1968, he was only sixty. In 1964 he had been an old soldier in *Doctor Zhivago,* which was just one of the many films he appeared in, the last being *A Bridge Too Far,* in which he played the church organist, and the film was released the same year as his death.

In late autumn I was taken out to dinner at Simpson's in The Strand by John Farrow, a producer who offered me the part of Buttons in *Cinderella* at the Intimate Theatre, Palmer's Green, near Tottenham. Over dinner we discussed how I would like to make my entrance and he suggested a back-projected film of a crazy car chase. When I got to the theatre I discovered either the man was a fantasist or a bullshitter, because the depth of the stage in this little theatre was no more than about twelve feet, and to make an entrance from another side of the stage one had to exit into the street at the back of the theatre to cross over.

When I got to know John better, I think it was bullshit rather than fantasy.

One night, in this rather rough and ready production, I was doing a front cloth gag which involved hurling my parcel filled with china about the stage. I kicked the parcel back to one of the Broker's Men, and knowing almost nothing about football, cried out, 'Up the Arsenal!' Chaos broke out. You could hear the boos of the Tottenham supporters from as far away as Bow Street Police Station, from where I thought they must be getting ready to send a riot squad to quell this mob of deranged toddlers. There was nothing for it other than to leave the stage and get on with the next number. I vowed never to mention football ever again.

John Farrow asked me to do him a favour. Would I drive to Redditch where his production of *Aladdin* was about to open at the Palace Theatre, and give the cast their salaries, as they should have been paid on the Friday? I agreed and drove up to this West Midlands town early on Sunday morning. When I got to the theatre, I found the cast despondent, and the director almost in tears. For their magical cave scene all they had was a free-standing fragment of scenery at centre stage, about six feet in length and about two feet high and called a ground row. And as if to add insult to injury, this mockery of Aladdin's bejewelled cavern had been badly painted with a smattering of flowers, as if a child had coloured it in. It was a disgrace and made me very angry. When I saw Farrow later in the week, and told him about the lack of scenery there, he shrugged it off. And then he told me that when *Aladdin* opened on the Monday there was a worse disaster. The musical director, although she could play keyboards perfectly, what no one knew was that she couldn't read music, and the principal girl had to sing an entire ballad to nothing but drum accompaniment. Clearly her memory had let her down and she couldn't remember the tune.

I was relieved when *Cinderella* closed.

Malcom and I had worked hard getting dates for a ten week tour of *Under Milk Wood*, and before the New Year we had eight of them confirmed, good dates with guaranteed sums paid to our production company which covered the costs of each date. It was a cast of eleven, including Malcolm and myself. Peter Denyer agreed to direct again. Our cast included Meredith Edwards as Captain Cat. He was a familiar face from such British films as *The Cruel Sea* and *Where No Eagles Fly*. We also cast David Lloyd Meredith, another Welsh actor, who played DS Evans in *Softly, Softly Task Force*. And having worked with Ian Masters in the feeble *Just Plain Murder,* we knew how good he really was, so he was cast as an excellent Mr Pugh and other roles. Apart from Meredith Edwards as Captain Cat and Ian Talbot as Narrator, everyone else played about four different roles, including Rosemary Faith who played Daisy Pratt in the fourth series of *Please Sir!*, June Lewis who played in two series of *Budgie* as Mrs Charlie Endell, Joan Blackham, my wife Zélie, and Tony Guilfoyle.

Although Peter Denyer directed the Stratford East production, he was not the best choice of director for this production. Peter could be extremely obstinate if he got a bee in his bonnet about something. He said he hated adults playing young children, and so he cut all the wonderful dialogue as Captain Cat listens to the children 'tumble and rhyme on the cobbles'.

This upset Meredith Edwards, and most of us agreed with him. So I and other members of the cast made it clear to Peter that we wanted Thomas's wonderful scene left in. But Peter said if it was left in he would walk out. Malcolm then said he would take over the direction, but Ian Talbot had little faith in Malcolm's direction and pleaded with me to get Peter to remain as director. In the end, we decided for Ian Talbot's sake to cut the children's scene, which satisfied Peter Denyer and he remained as director.

What I think we should have done was wait until Peter Denyer finished his direction and returned home, then reinstated Dylan Thomas's children's scene without his knowledge. Then, if he turned up at a later stage to see the play, and if he had any objections, we could have made it clear that we were the producers and there was nothing he could do about it. Again, hindsight always tells you what you should have done. But there are no rewind buttons.

We played some great dates, including Bath Theatre Royal, Cardiff New Theatre, Leeds Grand and the Manchester Palace. Unfortunately, our actors were contracted to do a ten week tour, and we had difficulty filling the last two dates. I can't even remember the penultimate date, I must have wiped it from my memory. All I can remember is the fact that we lost money because we had no choice but to accept box-office splits on the last two dates. And 70 per cent of nothing is nothing. Our final death-knell came at the Ashton Theatre, Lytham St Anne's, where we played to ridiculously thin houses. Not only that, but my marriage to Zélie had gone belly-up (my fault entirely) even as we embarked on the tour.

But life has its ups and downs and there were some great moments on the tour. During a week at the MacRobert Centre in Stirling, Mike Grayson the theatre administrator, gave us a cheque for our two-thousand on the Thursday, with which to pay the cast and stage management salaries. In those days, it was an Equity rule that all their members must be paid in cash no later than noon every Friday. The cheque was made out to cash, and Grayson came with us to the bank. The cashier recognised Malcolm and me and asked if she could have our autographs. We gave her our signatures, and then as we waited to cash the cheque, she said, 'Could I see some proof of identity please?'

We also got some rave reviews on the tour, but I'm not sure it made up for the loss of money during those last two dates.

Even though my agent, Keith Whitall, knew we had lost money on the tour, he realized we wouldn't have faced a loss had we contracted the actors for an eight week tour, because the first eight weeks were guaranteed. Keith joined Stonebridge Productions, and we set about planning a tour of the Ray Cooney and Tony Hilton farce *One For The Pot* which Malcolm directed. I was cast as Hickory Wood, playing opposite Bob Grant as Charlie Barnet. Not only was Bob well-known as bus conductor Jack from *On the Buses*, he was an extremely experienced comedy actor and farceur, and became a great hit in the theatre when he played Foreign Secretary George Brown in *Mrs Wilson's Diary*. Pamela Vezey, we cast as Amy Hardcastle, who had recently played Billy Fisher's long-suffering mother in the television version of *Billy Liar*. Jenny Lee-Wright was cast as her daughter Cynthia Hardcastle. Jenny had appeared in dozens of comedy shows with comedians like Morecombe and Wise and Frankie Howerd, and in the 1980s she gave up acting and became a full-time Foley Artist.[2]

The part of my girlfriend Winnie went to Rosemary Faith, with whom I had worked briefly in one episode of the fourth series of *Please Sir!*. Ivor Salter was a wonderful flamboyant Jugg the butler. Ivor had been a regular in the soap opera *Market in Honey Lane,* an earlier version of *EastEnders* in many ways and made at the same studio complex in Elstree. Ivor also appeared in two episodes of *The Fenn Street Gang* and was in the ill-fated *In For a Penny,* the sitcom Mark Stuart attempted to disavow until we kept reminding him of it.

One can only marvel at the mechanics and trickery of co-writer Ray Cooney's well-constructed farce. In Act One I played the gormless Billy Hickory Wood, and then his twin brother Rupert, an upper-class one, until an Irish one appears, making the Hickory Woods triplets. This meant that because of the way the play was constructed with hidden exits and entrances, we had to employ two assistant stage managers who could be used as doubles, when one of their arms appeared from behind a sofa or hidden in a cupboard. Trevor Gray, one of the ASMs, his timing was spot on, but the other one, known as Rory Allison (we later discovered his real name was David Smith) was a wannabe method actor. At one stage I demanded a brandy from my twin hiding in the cupboard, then a glass of brandy shot out, handed to me by my double, at this stage played by Rory. I then asked for soda and immediately

---

2   Foley is the art of reproducing everyday sound effects that are added to films, and other media, in post-production. These reproduced sounds are named after sound-effects artist Jack Foley.

a jet of soda squirted me in the face. Or it should have done. Unfortunately, Rory paused for too long, and timing in farce has to be perfect. A one second delay and the comedy falls flat on its face. When I told Rory to speed it up, he offered the excuse that this was unrealistic, and he wouldn't have had time for the character to react and reach for the soda syphon. Rory was hard work.

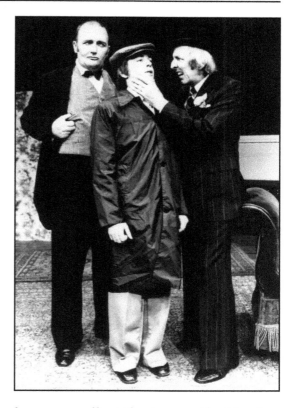

Unlike Bob Grant who was a joy to work with. A great comedy actor, his timing was brilliant, and he invented loads of funny business, essential for well-paced farce. And the rest of the cast were excellent, so that Malcolm, Keith and I were pleased with the result. We played many excellent theatres on the Number One touring circuit, but there was one gap in our tour we needed to fill, and when we were pencilling-in our dates six months ago, we gave the Civic Theatre, Broxbourne, a try. At the time of the booking, the theatre hadn't yet opened for business. But the manager booked us on a £2,000 guarantee and everything was agreed. He even went ahead and mentioned our show in *The Stage* newspaper, and his own press release said *One For The Pot* would be coming to the new theatre at Broxbourne later in the year. But as time wore on, we still hadn't received a contract. Not even as our tour kicked off, despite us ringing him, when we were told he was either not in the office or busy. On about our second date, which I think was the Wolverhampton Grand Theatre, we phoned the Broxbourne Theatre to ask what their poster requirements were, to be told the manager had left, hadn't been replaced, and if we didn't have a contract, then that was that.

We panicked and told the councillors we spoke to that we had proof that an agreement existed between us and their errant manager who seemed to have disappeared. Malcolm and I rose early the following morning and drove from Wolverhampton to Broxbourne. We sat outside the council chambers while councillors grilled us. We showed them *The Stage* cutting, which we pointed out came from them and not us. We also showed them our diary entries, proof of our phone calls with their theatre manager. They agreed that we had a deal with Broxbourne, despite not having a signed contract. They then said as there had been no publicity for our show, could we do just three performances for half the money. No, we said, we still had to pay the same salaries to our actors and pay for the removal lorry (not Eden's!) to transport our set, plus all the other expenses. They disappeared back inside the chambers to discuss this, returning soon afterwards when they agreed to pay the full amount, but still wanted only three performances from Thursday to Saturday.

Back at Wolverhampton after the show, Malcolm and I celebrated that night, as did the actors who would have three days off with pay later in the tour. And it taught us a valuable lesson. A verbal agreement is worth the paper it's printed on!

Often when touring, actors need to fill their days, and too much time spent in a pub can be dangerous when there is an evening performance to get through. So, depending on the city or town, sightseeing becomes essential for killing time. I feel as if I've traipsed through almost every famous cathedral in the country. And I have spent many of my touring afternoons in a cinema. It was during the *One For The Pot* tour that I happened to catch *Confessions of a Pop Performer* with Robin Askwith again as the trouser-dropping Timmy Lea. But what I didn't know was that Peter Cleall and Carol Hawkins were in it. As I was often in touch with Peter, he hadn't mentioned being in this film. I wondered if he had kept quiet about it because it was voted joint worst British film of 1975 by *Sight and Sound* magazine, tying with *The Rocky Horror Picture Show*? However, there was one line in it that caused me to guffaw. It was delivered by Rita Webb, who played Fanny's mother in the film, and when she said, 'Have you seen my Fanny?', I imagined Deryck Guyler cringing as he prepared himself for another profane assault by his bête noire.

I used to enjoy having a drink with Bob and his wife Kim. One night while sitting in a pub, I happened to ask him about his programme biography and his reference to working as a frozen food salesman. He laughed and told me it was a total disaster. As he tried to sell frozen vegetables to grocers in Norfolk, they all laughed at him, waved towards the distant fields and said, 'We got all the vegetables we need growing out there.'

But he eventually capitalized on this misfortune and wrote about it in a radio play which was accepted by the BBC.

Bob was a heavy drinker, although he was careful not to drink much before a show. But sometimes if he had to drive, and may have been over the limit, Kim sat in the back of his Audi, and then he opened the glove compartment and donned a chauffeur's hat. (I used this as a device for my main character in my fictional book *Muscle,* published in 2013.)

In the evening after a performance, as is quite common when touring, many members of a company will dine out, usually at a late-night Chinese or Indian restaurant, and the *One For The Pot* company was no exception. Jenny Lee-Wright's boyfriend at that time was Rocky Taylor, a stuntman who holds the record for being the oldest stuntman in Britain, with 35 years as a stunt performer and 20 years as a stunt co-ordinator. We met Rocky early on in the tour, a very gentle and affable Londoner. But he was a trifle possessive where Jenny was concerned. Wherever we went to dine after a show, he would find out which restaurant we were at, and in those days long before mobile phones, she would be called away from her meal to take Rocky's call on the restaurant phone, a call which sometimes went on for more than 45 minutes, ruining her meal.

On a more positive note, however, the tour brought together our ASM Trevor Gray and Rosemary Faith, a romance that eventually ended up with wedding bells.

At the end of the tour, I stayed in touch with Bob, and we were both going to appear in a farce he had written, putting it on in collaboration with Martin Williams at the Cardiff New Theatre. We decided to name our production company Theatre in The Seventies and had a laugh when we thought of shortening this to an acronym. Unfortunately, Martin Williams died of a sudden heart attack, and so without the backing of the New Theatre, we had to abandon plans to tour Bob's play.

(I was much saddened to learn of Bob Grant's suicide in 2003 from carbon monoxide poisoning. I thought he was a highly underrated actor, and his excellent performing talents became overlooked as he aged, leading to his deep depression. And I couldn't help wondering if his wife Kim was with him, or had perhaps left him, which may have contributed to his depression.)

When *One For The Pot* ended, and we had an evaluation of our success or failure at Keith's office in Richmond, we discovered the show had made a loss of £200 after a twelve week tour, but we had employed a cast of nine, plus the two ASM doubles, and a Stage and Deputy Stage Manager. This encouraged

Keith to carry on with the next project that I tried to talk him out of, *The Trail of The Lonesome Pine*, which cost him a bust-making loss of £17,000 the following year.

But first I was offered, along with Malcolm, a pantomime, *Babes In The Wood* at the Gaumont Cinema, Doncaster, starring Cy Grant as Alan A Dale. Grant was well known for providing topical calypso numbers for the BBC news show *Tonight*. Originally from Guyana, in 1941 he joined the RAF, became a Flight Lieutenant navigator, and on his third mission was shot down over the Netherlands. He was captured and spent the next two years in the prisoner of war camp Stalag Luft III until the allied liberation.

Another company member with wartime experience was Edwin Braden, our musical director, who provided mid-show music for *Round the Horne* and *Beyond Our Ken*, as Eddie Braden and the Hornblowers. Malcolm, Eddie and I stayed in the same hotel, and Eddie, after he usually topped his breakfast tea up with a generous measure of whisky, regaled us with his stories. He served in the army during World War II and was in the North Africa campaign. He told us that one Christmas, their unit came across an abandoned village in which there was a large vat containing red wine. It was apparently a rule that soldiers serving in the desert must never waste water from their canteens, but as it was Christmas Day, and there was a well in the village with enough water to refill everyone's canteens, a special dispensation was granted from the CO that every soldier would be allowed to empty their canteen and fill up with wine to celebrate. Pretty soon all the wine was drunk. At the bottom of the vat it was discovered there were belt buckles, gold teeth, and metal buttons. It looked as if bodies had been disposed of in the vat, and everything that wasn't metal had been eaten away over time by the wine. Eddie chuckled and said, 'Mind you, that wine had a fine body to it!'

The pantomime was produced by Alexander Bridge of West End Artists and directed by Michael J. Smith, who knew as much about directing a show as I know about the laws of thermodynamics. And we only had about eight days' rehearsal. We began rehearsals in Doncaster on Monday 15 December. Friday came and went, and we weren't paid, but we were told that because the production company had so many other productions running concurrently, they didn't have anyone able to make the trip to Doncaster to pay us. Instead, we were offered two weeks' money the following Friday after the show had opened. We should have been suspicious, but as we were playing to large audiences, we assumed everything was above board.

In the wings every night, as we waited to make our entrance, Malcolm and I spluttered as we watched the actor playing Will Scarlet saying his lines as he accidentally discovers the red tunic that gives him his name. There was an error in the script, and rather than tell him so that he could correct it, we thought it much more fun to hear his camp delivery every night as he said, 'Well, here is a fine jerking.'

Also, we became great friends with Bernie Higginson, the pit drummer, and the three of us hardly stopped laughing during this disaster-filled show.

The following Friday, our next pay day when we had been promised our money, was Boxing Day, and we were told as the banks were shut no one could be paid until they opened. By now we all knew something was very wrong with this company. But they promised us full payment by Friday the 1st January, another bank holiday when the banks would be shut.

On Friday, an Equity representative arrived on the scene, who turned out to be less than useless and we all performed the show that evening. The show was scheduled to run for another two weeks until January 17, but the Gaumont Cinema management said West End Artists had gone bankrupt, and they had no option but to end the show on Saturday, despite the advance bookings being excellent. During a heated company meeting, most of the cast suggested it would be awful to cancel and disappoint all the kiddies and parents who had booked tickets for Saturday. It was a show must go on attitude, even though none of us had seen a single penny in three weeks. I have to admit I was one of the few in the company who said we were within our rights not to perform, but when it came to a vote I was outnumbered.

Following our two final (unpaid) performances, the Gaumont Cinema advertised a film opening on Monday 4 January. *The Towering Inferno*.

I had no cash and no cheques left in my chequebook, so how was I able to get home? I had heard somewhere that provided you have all the account details etc., and a bank guarantee card, you can write a cheque out on ordinary paper and this will be legally binding. I wasn't certain it would work, so what I did was drive into a petrol station, fill up the tank, then explain my predicament to the cashier. I wrote out my cheque on half a sheet of A4 paper, and it worked. The payment was honoured.

During our time in Doncaster, and visiting a pub after the performance, a record that had reached the charts and was playing on the pub juke box was Laurel and Hardy singing 'The Trail of The Lonesome Pine'. It was lightbulb moment and I thought why not produce a western pantomime of the same name? Same format as a traditional panto: principal girl, boy, dame, pantomime horse etc., but set in the Wild West, with Billy the Kid as the villain. When I shared this concept with everyone, I was assured it was a brilliant idea. And when I returned to the south east and told my agent Keith Whitall about it, he was so enthusiastic, he immediately began making plans.

Having decided to tour it in the summer, we hoped to get children clamouring to see this entertainment during the school holidays. Then suddenly, like the bright idea bulb, another sign: a neon warning in my brain. Perhaps this might not be such a good idea after all. Staring self-doubt in the face, I had visions of a cowboy pantomime with hordes of children gaping in bewilderment. This was an unknown quantity, unexplored territory. Would audiences expect more traditional fare?

As Keith was wholly financing the project, I suggested that maybe we ought to put on a safer and less costly production. I attempted to persuade him to mount a production of Ibsen's *Ghosts* instead, touring it to university theatres where we could ask for box-office guarantees against loss. But Keith was sold on producing a glitzy show with songs and routines and chorus girls in dazzling costumes.

Although I had written the show very much in the pantomime tradition, as this was Wild West territory we decided early on that the principal boy ought to be played by a male, and we put our heads together to find a suitable named-actor to play the leading role of Cheyenne. They were showing repeats of the original *Batman* series on television, so we tried to tempt Adam West, and even went as far as to buy lunch for his UK agent, who then glibly informed us that West was always far too busy appearing in lucrative conventions to consider touring and tried to interest us in Burt Ward, Batman's Robin, instead. But on questioning him about Ward's availability, it became clear this agent didn't represent the Robin actor and was probably just winging it, liked talking big, and enjoying a free lunch.

Next, we tried to interest Peter Noone of Herman's Hermits, who had hits in the sixties with songs like 'No Milk Today' and 'Something is Happening'. After making the initial enquiry via his agent, Peter Noone rang me from his home in the South of France to politely decline the offer, saying had it been a straight play and not a pantomime he might have been interested. Probably leaving his options open, in case we produced serious plays, and the Herman's Hermits singer might be cast as the next Hamlet or Macbeth.

When we did eventually cast our lead actor, he turned out to be perfect for the role. Johnny More was a talented impressionist who had appeared in *Now Who Do You Do?* on television. He had a great voice, and his Frank

Sinatra was one of the best. When we met him, Keith and I hit it off with him immediately, and he was enthusiastic about the production. When we mentioned him doing a song sheet, bringing some of the children in the audience up onto the stage at the end of the show, he suggested a table could be set with various props – a fez, beret, bowler hat and cane, and the kids were invited to do their impressions of Tommy Cooper, Frank Spencer or Charlie Chaplin. This worked brilliantly and became one of the highlights of the show.

We opened at the Southend Cliffs Pavilion, with Malcolm having done the lighting design, and this theatre was one of the few dates where we had negotiated a guaranteed fee, so even though the houses were not remarkable, we were able to cover our costs. But that infamous summer of 1976 turned into a scorcher, and few parents wanted to fork out money for their children to sit in a theatre when their offspring were happy to play on the beach for free. It was the plague-of-ladybirds summer, and despite rave reviews from the critics, we were crucified at the box office and Keith lost a small fortune.

It was such a shame, nothing we could do about the burning climate, and the audiences that did see the show loved it. And we had a good cast. Well, with one exception. But there's always one, isn't there?

His name was Robin Stewart, and he had turned up to start rehearsals two days late, with barely an apology. Robin was well known as Sidney James's son in *Bless This House,* and he partnered me as a comedy duo, Butch and Sundance, a western version of the traditional Broker's Men. He was a good-looking young man and had a sneering swagger to match. He talked big, and cadged lifts off some of the cast to get to each venue. When Johnny More asked him why he wasn't driving a car on tour, this elicited a 'My Merc's got a hairline fracture in the gearbox.'

Not long after the show opened, Bernie Higginson, with whom Malcolm and I had worked in the ill-fated pantomime at Doncaster, and was again our pit drummer, talked to Malcolm and me about Robin. He said, 'The bloke can't act, can't sing and can't dance. What can he do? He's nothing but a knob end.' From that moment on, we always referred to Robin as 'Knob End'.

During the third date of the tour, there was not enough money in the box-office to pay the cast and Keith had to forward cheques. The only person who had a problem with this was Robin, who protested that it was awkward as he banked with the Bank of Montreal. Johnny flashed him a sidelong look and said wryly, 'I might have known you wouldn't have banked with the Co-op Bank at Blackburn, Robin.'

Playing Dame Diamond Lil, the saloon bar entertainer, was Barry Howard, who supplied his own glitzy frocks as he used to partner John Inman when they played Ugly Sisters together. Barry became well-known on television in the 1980s when he played Barry Stuart-Hargreaves in *Hi-de-Hi* as husband and dancing partner to his snooty wife Yvonne, played by Diane Holland.

Barry didn't drive, so I gave him a lift to most of our venues on the tour. During our first journey he confided to me that he could never really like anyone who lacked talent, adding that he had little time for Knob-End.

When we played Nottingham Theatre Royal, Robin was visited one night by two detectives, who spent much time interviewing him in his dressing room. In the pub after the show, we noticed he had a slight bruise on his cheek, and he told us he had been assaulted by one of the doormen when he went clubbing the previous night, and he was now bringing a charge of criminal assault against them and would be returning to Nottingham after the tour was over to appear in court as plaintiff, when he would see that yobbo punished for his unruly behaviour. We all took the story with a pinch of salt.

Our final venue on this financial ruin was at the Theatre Royal, Norwich. Prior to the show one night, I called in at the nearest pub where some of the young cast members liked to have a pre-show drink. Warwick Evans, who was then only 22, and some other younger members of the cast were discussing their careers, and how they were just getting started. I asked them

if they had seen the six o'clock news. None of them had, so I casually dropped into the conversation that the government was bringing back conscription, and anyone under the age of 26 would be called up for two years' national service. I left them to mull this over and headed for the theatre.

And then it was back down to earth as we faced the last night of the show with a devastating loss of money forcing Keith Whitall out of the business. And I heard he had a nervous breakdown not long afterwards. 1976 turned out to be our *annus horribilus*, although that Latin phrase from the Queen's 1992 speech reminded me that the year came to a positive end on 25 December when *Please Sir!* was shown on ITV immediately following the Queen's Commonwealth speech at 3 p.m.

In 1998, I bumped into Warwick Evans in Windsor as he was returning from Bill Kenwright's office where he went to collect a Gold Disc for his part as Narrator in *Blood Brothers*. Over coffee he told me he had dined out on the bringing back National Service wind-up over the years, and still laughs about it, although he wasn't laughing at the time, having spent most of the two-hour show having nightmares about square bashing.

Penny-Pinching Producers

In 1975 Charles Vance, a rather flamboyant actor/manager, who often strutted about with Henry Irving's walking cane, had employed me just for one week's rehearsal, and one week's performance at the Hull New Theatre in *The Creeper*, a play by Pauline Macauley about a wealthy eccentric man who advertises for a young companion, directed by Malcolm McFee. I enjoyed working with Malcolm again, who was always so calm and thoughtful, and we got along well together. So it looked as if all of us in *The Fenn Street Gang* would become friends and our paths would cross many times for years to come, but not necessarily through work, although I always paid particular attention to the many film and TV appearances of my *Please Sir!* mates.

Penny Spencer was soon hunting alien invaders in Gerry Anderson's *UFO* and many years later I saw her in a Reg Varney vehicle, a feature film called *The Best Pair of Legs in The Business*. Peter Denyer I often enjoyed watching in the series *Dear John* as the hapless Ralph, and even more so when he was the gay man in the series *Agony*, starring Maureen Lipman as the agony aunt. And Peter must have felt a certain amount of freedom playing that part as a gay man himself. His gay partner in the series was played by Jeremy Bulloch, although Jeremy is not gay in real life. I had been at Corona Academy with Jeremy and hadn't bumped into him for many years until I attended a convention at a holiday camp near Great Yarmouth in 2006, but I'm not certain about the year. I sat next to him at the convention, signing copies of my first published book, *Each Man Kills*, and *Please Sir!* photographs, while Jeremy autographed photographs of himself as the masked Boba Fett from the *Star Wars* films *The Empire Strikes Back* and *The Return of The Jedi*. This was the first convention I had ever attended and I was surprised to see fans dressing up as their favourite characters. I spotted at least three Dr Who Tom Bakers, and when I went to the loo I was slightly unnerved to find myself standing at a urinal next to an Ewok.

Carol Hawkins for many years played comedy roles in films and on television, appearing on several occasions in *The Two Ronnies* and she was in a memorable Christmas episode of *Porridge*. Her two *Carry On* films were *Carry On Abroad* and *Carry On Behind*. Liz Gebhardt, as far as I know was the only ex-5C actor to work in another television production written by Esmonde and Larbey. This was *Football Crazy* which was a children's television sitcom. But the drama I remember her most from was in *The Naked Civil Servant* starring John Hurt as Quentin Crisp, with Liz as his art student friend. Liz's husband, Ian Talbot, was artistic director of Regent's Park Open Air Theatre, and throughout the 1980s I managed to attend many productions whenever Liz was there, as Ian always gave us complimentary tickets. In one of the productions I attended, *The Two Gentlemen of Verona*, Launce was played by Peter Bayliss, and during one of his long dialogues, his dog Crab (played by a real dog), could see tiny little midges flying about, which we the audience couldn't see, and Crab got loads of laughs whenever he snapped at these invisible things. When we met Peter after the performance I asked him if he minded being upstaged by the dog. He laughed and said the dog was brilliant and that he and Crab had a certain rapport. And then he suggested what he always did whenever I bumped into him, that LWT ought to write a new *Please Sir!* series in which we ex-5C actors play the parents of a new class. The last time I saw Peter was when he played Doolittle the dustman in *My Fair Lady* in the West End, and when I went backstage to see him, again he suggested they ought to revive the series with us as parents, and I said, 'Don't you mean grandparents, Peter?'

Peter Cleall appeared in many television productions in the 1980s, including the collaboration between Johnny Speight and Alan Simpson, *Spooner's Patch*. And whenever Peter worked in the theatre I would often go and see him. I especially remember seeing his performance as Dan in *Night Must Fall* by Emlyn Williams, in which he was excellent. And sometime in the '90s I got to play his wife. Yes, really! And I have the photo to prove it. This was at the Nightingale Theatre in Brighton, and it was in the Caryl Churchill play *Cloud Nine*. The play was directed by Brian Capron, who *Coronation Street* viewers will remember as serial killer Richard Hillman.

In 1979 Charles Vance decided to tour *The Creeper*, with Bill Simpson in the leading role, and again he offered me the part of Maurice Morris the young ex-shop assistant, who becomes his menacing companion, with Malcolm co-directing. The play was being produced in association with another impresario, John Newman of Newpalm Productions. (Actors feeling hard done by, or having a bitch about the company, often referred to it as Napalm Productions.)

John Newman directed the show for a week's rehearsal in London prior to a fortnight's rehearsal in Harrogate, where the show would run for two weeks before going on tour. When Charles Vance came to a rehearsal, he didn't like Newman's direction, and insisted on redirecting it at Harrogate, then left Malcolm to pick up the pieces.

Bill Simpson played the title role in *Doctor Finlay's Casebook* for many years on BBC Television. I liked Bill, got on very well with him, but he was an alcoholic and he never got to grips with the dialogue. When we rehearsed in Harrogate we soon discovered we had to start rehearsals early and finish at lunchtime in order to accommodate Bill's drinking habit – always a half and a half (a half pint of beer with a large whisky chaser). Which was not good news when it came to performances, even if he did have a nap in the afternoon. My character was shy, nervous and diffident, and it was Bill as Edward Kimberley who had the bulk of the dialogue. Often in performance he left me alone on stage while he walked into the wings to find out what his next lines were from the deputy stage manager, and I had to improvise what an introverted young man would do when left alone in a wealthy man's living room.

While we were in Harrogate, John Newman telephoned me and said the company hadn't got a company manager joining the production until the tour kicked off at Edinburgh Lyceum, and would I please act as an unpaid company manager for Harrogate and mentioned there would be large drink in it for me. I accepted, didn't mind doing him a favour, and the *quid pro quo* of the arrangement was what I guessed might be a bottle of champagne or brandy.

At the Lyceum on Monday 7 May we had a press call. Less than a week before, on 3 May 1979, it was the general election and Margaret Thatcher was voted in as the first female prime minister. For the press call I wore a pin-striped suit, a white shirt and black tie. The bait was set. Sure enough, one of the journalists asked me, 'Are you in mourning?'

'Only politically,' I replied.

This was quoted in *The Scotsman*. Unfortunately, I wasn't credited with the quip. It was reported as having been said by a cast member of *The Creeper*. When I confessed to Bill that I was responsible for the remark, he told me he was a card-carrying Conservative, frequently attended his Conservative Club whenever he was in Scotland, and he now worried that fellow members might think he was responsible for the comment. But there was a twinkle in his eye when he told me, and I suspect he enjoyed the idea of stirring things up.

After the first night's performance I approached John Newman at the bar, who didn't look as if he was about to thrust a bottle into my arms. 'What about that large drink you promised me?' I reminded him.

'Did I say large?' he replied.

I knew there would be no thank you bottle, so I ordered a large gin and dry martini and took pleasure as I watched the colour drain from his face. Bill, thinking the producer was buying a large drink for everyone ordered a large malt whisky, and the other three members of the cast and two stage management also ordered large drinks. The round cost him nearly fifteen pounds, far more than if he had bought me that bottle.

Despite his heavy drinking creating difficulties in performance, I got along well with Bill. He had personal problems and he often confided in me that he was deeply troubled by his marriage to Tracy Reed, Sir Carol Reed's daughter.

I find it difficult remembering the order of dates for this tour. Possibly we played Liverpool next, followed by the Sunderland Empire Theatre. There was a backstage bar at this venue and it was to be Bill's undoing one night. I was alone on stage at the end of the first act, waiting for him to enter, when he would gesture for me to deal the cards for a game of cribbage as the curtain falls. As I sat anticipating his entrance, the double doors of the set rattled. At first I thought the doors had jammed. Then more frantic rattling. To my horror I saw the scenery began to shake. An angry exclamation from behind the set, and then the doors caved inwards and crashed onto the stage, exposing the backstage wall. An angry, red-faced Doctor Finlay staggered forward and shouted, 'That is the end of Act One!'

The curtain fell quickly. In his drunken stupor, Bill had forgotten that the doors opened inwards towards the back of the stage and thinking they had jammed, and that someone else was to blame, he pushed them forwards using savage brute force. Following this incident, the management complained to the production company and his agent, and a soberer Edward Kimberley performed at our next date, which was the Yvonne Arnaud Theatre, Guildford. This close to London, Bill had to be on his best behaviour.

It was while at this venue we were asked to appear at a charity summer fair in Guildford. Also appearing at this event was Anna Bergman, Ingmar Bergman's daughter, who appeared in *Mind Your Language* at the time. John

Newman, with his other half of the production company, Daphne Palmer, came to see the show, and suggested they have dinner afterwards with Bill and Anna Bergman. Bill told me later that he was expected to share payment of the bill with John Newman, until Anna Bergman shamed the producer into paying by saying in an astounded voice: 'You are his producer, and you are not even paying for dinner?'

The next venue involved flying to Belfast, to appear at the Riverside Theatre, Coleraine. It was at the New University of Ulster, drinking in the common room bar there, that I got to know R. D. Smith (Reggie), an ex-BBC producer, who was Professor Emeritus at the university. He came to see our show several times, was fascinated by it, and hugely complimentary about my performance. And Bill was now comparatively sober and getting through it without many cock-ups.

Reggie Smith, was an interesting man, flamboyant and friendly, with a great history which I later discovered. He was married to novelist Olivia Manning, and she later wrote about their wartime experiences as they escaped Nazi occupation across Europe in the fictionalised *The Fortunes of War*, and Reggie became the protagonist Guy Pringle, played by Kenneth Branagh in the BBC series in 1987.

The final venue on the tour was the Nell Gwynne Theatre in Hereford. As co-producer Charles Vance turned up for the penultimate performance and asked if he could join our farewell meal at an Italian restaurant after the show. We took this to mean that he wouldn't be paying, which we all thought was fair enough as we were five in the cast and two stage management. The waiter gave him the bill at the end of the evening and he told us what our equal share was. We all coughed up. But he had miscalculated the pennies column and in a staggering display of miserly behaviour he said we owed him an extra twenty-six pence each. Astonished, we dug into our pockets for loose change to make up the bill.

Clearly, he was from the same mould as John Newman.

Malcolm McFee now worked as an assistant for impresario Malcolm Knight of Malcolm Knight Productions, not to be confused with another Malcolm Knight who is secretary of the CAA (Club for Acts and Actors) in Covent Garden. Malcolm suggested me for Knight's next tour, which was a revival of the Lionel Bart musical *Fings Ain't Wot They Used T'Be*, playing the part of Red-Hot, a small-time thief, a character who has one solo musical number. The musical was set in a 1950s illegal gambling club in Soho, with a large cast of characters made up of villains and prostitutes. Malcolm Knight agreed to cast me providing I signed up to do his pantomime at the Gordon Craig Theatre, Stevenage, at Christmas. Knowing little about the producer at this stage, I readily agreed, as this would give me employment from late summer into the next decade.

The musical opened at Reading's Hexagon Theatre. Frank Norman, who wrote the book of the show attended with Lionel Bart. I was in the front of house before the show and I could see they were both well-oiled. Later on, I heard they had bailed out during the first half, gone to the bar, then disappeared.

During rehearsals I heard much gossip about producer Malcolm Knight, none of it good, but I always believe in take as you find. But on tour I soon found out why the diminutive producer was known as 'The Poison Dwarf'. When he occasionally appeared, he often showed a great deal of interest in some of the young women in the cast, and if that interest wasn't reciprocated, he bullied them and made their lives a misery. If you spent much time in The Poison Dwarf's company, you felt like taking a shower afterwards. And not long into the tour I heard Malcolm lost his temper and resigned from the company by grabbing Knight round the lapels and pushing him up against the wall.

Despite working for Knight, it turned out to be an exciting and intriguing show, and most of the cast got on well during the twelve week tour. Following a Saturday night performance at Edinburgh King's Theatre, as we all packed up our things in the dressing rooms, over the show relay system came the stage doorman's voice wishing us all the best of luck next week at Kirkcaldy. Putting on Private Frazer's voice from *Dad's Army*, he warned 'Your doomed. You're all doomed.' And as we left by the stage door, he reiterated, 'They're a funny lot in Fife.'

And how right he was. Remembering the incident with Peter and Malcolm in the function room at the hotel, I wasn't surprised when a mysterious bomb scare halted the show one night. Possibly the hoax call was made by one of the God-fearing citizens of Kirkcaldy, upset at seeing a musical about villains and prostitutes.

About halfway through the tour, Pat Carlile, one of the ensemble players in the show became my girlfriend. When we performed at Bournemouth, we met the *It Ain't Half Hot, Mum* cast, who were doing a summer season there. Drinking with Melvyn Hayes and Windsor Davies after the show, they invited me and Pat to a free buffet supper and drinks at a hotel on Thursday night but asked us to keep it quiet from the rest of our company as they couldn't invite loads of people. After our Thursday night show, the two of us joined Melvyn and Windsor at the hotel, and sure enough we could order whatever drinks we liked, and there was a great table laid out with a buffet supper. Then Melvyn whispered to me, 'There's someone I'd like you to meet, David. Can I borrow you for a minute?' He led me through a door, and suddenly I was standing on a stage in a spotlight in front of a large audience, and a DJ introduced me as Frankie Abbott.

The cast of *Ain't Half Hot* appeared there every Thursday to raise money for charity. Melvyn thought it was a good gag to put me on the spot like that, and I immediately switched to performance mode, using this joke I always kept up my sleeve:

'I expect you've been wondering what I've been up to since *Fenn Street Gang* ended. I've been working as a road sweeper. Well paid it was. Three hundred quid a week and I only had to sweep one road. It was the M25!'

Melvyn admitted afterwards that I handled it well.

The final date on the *Fings* tour was at the Swansea Grand Theatre, the first week in December. And because there were scenes in the show in which Red-Hot didn't appear, I was thrilled to climb that ladder, knock on the hatch, and peer through at skirting board level to buy a beer like a thirsty rodent.

Welsh winters are commonly wet, windy, and freezing cold, as I had suffered one working in pantomime at Porthcawl the previous year. But during that final December week of the *Fings* tour, Wales was blessed with freak sunshine and a high temperature, and some of us went walking along the sands at beautiful Rhossili Bay without overcoats.

My little car, which had taken us everywhere, including Scotland, was as knackered as I was, and the day after I returned to my flat at Crystal Palace, it collapsed and died. Which meant I had to commute by train to Stevenage. I managed to get through the Poison Dwarf's pantomime – I swear to you I can't even remember what the subject was now – in which the lead was played by Alan Randall, who did George Formby impressions and played musical instruments. His speciality act went on for a good twenty minutes, giving bored children an opportunity to misbehave. It reminded me of the apocryphal story of a panto introduction to a speciality instrumental act: 'Shipwrecked, lost and far from home, I'll play upon my xylophone.'

Frankie Becomes Elvis

Early in 1980 my agent sent me to Elstree Studios for an interview for the film of *George and Mildred*. I met with producer Roy Skeggs, and director Peter Frazer-Jones. I wasn't asked to read anything and I came away wondering if I had got the part or not, but by the time I got back to my flat in Crystal Palace they had come through with an offer. Apparently, the part had come about because Andrew Mitchell, producer of the *Please Sir!* film, had recommended me to Skeggs because the part of Elvis was so like that of Frankie Abbott. Pat and I celebrated that night with champagne and fish and chips.

Prior to shooting I was unable to attend the film's read-through because I was already engaged to do a three-day shoot for a Heineken commercial in Italy. The director was John Crome, and he had already used me in two commercials. The second being the beer-drinking yob luring Joanna Lumley to the Whitechapel bar, so presumably he was not fazed by my insobriety during that shoot.

The ad was shot in Genoa, and every night after the day's shoot, we were driven in unit cars to a restaurant where much was eaten and drunk. It was the first time I had tasted pasta with pesto sauce, which was delicious, and a speciality of the area. One night after dinner, the cars set off in a convoy back to the hotel. The first car went ahead, and was stopped by the police, who wanted to test the driver for alcohol consumption. But the rest of the unit cars, probably another six, surrounded them. Outnumbered, the police shrugged and drove off. Another sensible Italian retreat!

I asked John Crome, who was the only other Brit on the shoot, why they went to the expense of getting an actor from the UK to do an easy commercial, where all I had to do was appear as a competitor in a walking race, much of it speeded up like a Benny Hill sketch. John told me that actors in Italy look down on commercials and treat acting as an art.

Good to have it pointed out that I was prostituting myself again.

Although the script for *George and Mildred,* written by Dick Sharples, was more farcical than the television series which was built around character, it gave me the opportunity to play a decent sized role in another feature film. Stratford Johns, always recognisable for his Detective Chief Superintendent Barlow in *Z Cars, Softly, Softly* and *Barlow,* was gangster Harry Pinto, my uncle. On the first day of the shoot I was introduced to Yootha Joyce, whose warmth immediately put me at ease. Although she was in an episode of *Fenn Street Gang*, it was one of the ones I wasn't contracted to appear in, so this was our first meeting. I had met Brian Murphy in 1974, when he rehearsed at the Northcott Theatre, Exeter, for the part of Archie Rice in *The Entertainer.* We were performing *The Lads from Fenn Street*, and he came out for a drink with us one night after our show.

Yootha was extremely professional and her performance was meticulous. There was nothing to indicate she had a drink problem. At first I didn't notice her absence from lunch. She always spent her hour's break in her dressing room, while Brian, Alan (Stratford's first name), Neil McCarthy, Sue Bond, and I ate our lunch at a large round table in the Elstree Studio restaurant. Neil played an Eastern European bodyguard in the film, and Sue Bond was Harry Pinto's mistress.

Because Yootha didn't join us for lunch didn't mean she was unsociable – far from it. Often we would have long conversations while they lit a scene. I remember her telling me she was in the process of buying her dream home on the River Dart in Devon. When she described its location to me, I knew it well, having been there many times on a visit from Torquay, going over on the one-car ferry to the pub on the opposite side of the river, where they sold fresh crab sandwiches.

One morning during filming at Elstree, I happened to ask Yootha what time the tea trolley was due. 'Not for a while yet,' she replied. 'Would you like something a bit more substantial?'

I looked at my watch. 'It's not ten o'clock yet.'

'But if it was a Sunday morning,' she pointed out, 'you would probably get up about eleven and be in the pub by twelve. And you probably got up before six today to get to the studio on time. That was more than four hours ago.'

I couldn't argue against such logic and accepted her offer. She whispered to her dresser, who went off and returned minutes later with a bottle of brandy concealed in her bag of knitting. Soon there was a party of us sitting around on canvas chairs sipping Yootha's brandy from disposable cups, including Brian and the director. But for us it was a one-off, and I got the impression that with Yootha it was habitual.

Brian's routine back then was that when he wasn't playing George, he wore a toupee. Perhaps it was an attempt to conceal his identity, as their George and Mildred characters were so popular they were often mobbed. Once, after a day's shoot, he asked me if I was going to the bar for a drink. I said I was and would knock on his dressing room door after getting changed. Knowing he had to get his wig on, I took my time getting changed. There was a knock on my door and to my surprise Brian was already waiting for me, his wig in place.

One morning I was standing around waiting to hit my mark in a scene, and I happened to glance at the large Mitchell camera about to start filming. At the side of this expensive piece of equipment was a brass plaque with some of the films the Mitchell had already shot engraved on it. Films like *Barry Lyndon, A Bridge Too Far* and *The Shining*. It amused me to think of *George and Mildred* being added to this list.

On location for a car scene on an army private road, I shared a Winnebago with Stratford Johns. It was a hot day, and mid-morning he instructed his driver to get a few beers from the back of his boot. Few! His driver returned with a 24-pack of Carlsberg Special Brew. Fortunately, all that was required of us that day was cowering in the back of a car, driven by a stunt man, while Harry Fowler fired a gun out of the window at a pursuing car.

'Bloody hell!' he said during a break in the filming. 'People would pay to do this, and we're being paid to do it.'

When the film was released, sadly, Yootha was already dead. For some time afterwards I thought about her describing to me her perfect home overlooking the River Dart, and I often wondered if she got there, if only for a short time.

Around this time we watched the second series of *Fawlty Towers* which were probably repeats as they were first aired the previous year. It was great to see Joan Sanderson as Mrs Alice Richards in the episode *Communication Problems* and also Richard Davies as Mr White in *The Kipper and The Corpse* episode. They were absolutely stunning, and I have watched them many times over the years and they still make me laugh. Years later, Dickie told me just the one episode of *Fawlty Towers* was one of the most lucrative productions he was ever involved in, simply because his one episode was repeated so often and was huge worldwide. Also, the BBC profile has this lovely line: 'stands up to this day as a jewel in the BBC's comedy crown...' Although I believe John Cleese has kept the rather sarcastic letter of rejection he received from the BBC when he first submitted it to them.

There was another *Please Sir!* connection bringing me employment soon after the *George and Mildred* film. Mark Stuart was now with Thames Television and produced the sitcom *Keep It In The Family,* written by Brian Cooke. Early in 1981 I happened to send him an idea I had for a sitcom and he asked me to call at Thames Television near Teddington Lock to see him. When I met him, he said that while he was not interested in my sitcom idea, might I instead be interested in writing for Brian Cooke's series, because the writer needed to farm it out to other writers as he had to spend time in the U.S.A. overseeing the sitcom for an American version, which became *Too Close For Comfort.* As VCRs had not yet become a huge market, Mark sat me in a viewing room and I watched three episodes before deciding I was capable of writing for these characters. I went home and wrote a couple of synopses and scene examples over the next few weeks and was duly commissioned to write them.

I enjoyed writing for Robert Gillespie, whose idiosyncratic performance as Dudley Rush, the mischievous cartoonist, was endearingly funny. Pauline Yates, played his wife Muriel, and she had a few years previously performed opposite Leonard Rossiter as his wife in *The Fall and Rise of Reginald*

Perrin. The Rushes daughters, who lived in the downstairs flat, were played by Stacy Dorning and Sabina Franklyn. I had seen Stacy in episodes of *The Adventures of Black Beauty*, and also worked with her father, Robert Dorning, who appeared in TV episodes too numerous to list, but one of them was an episode of *Fenn Street Gang.*

Sabina was the daughter of the well-known actor William Franklyn, and she had appeared in *Basil the Rat*, the final episode of *Fawlty Towers.* Welsh

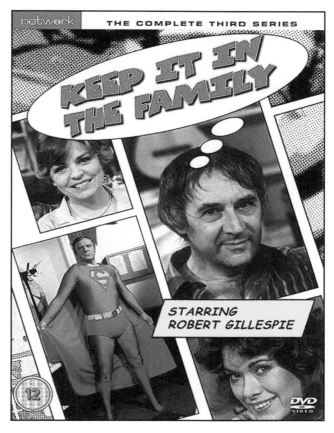

actor Glyn Houston played Duncan, Dudley's stoical and sometimes crabby boss. I loved writing for Glyn's character, and I had previously worked with him in a BBC Radio 4 version of *Under Milk Wood*, in which he played First Voice, and I played Dai Bread, Sinbad Sailors and Jack Black. I also worked with Glyn's brother, Donald Houston in Disney's *The Prince and The Pauper*, in which he played the villainous John Canty and I was his henchman.

Working on my first episode *A Game of No Chance* was thrilling, especially when Mark very kindly invited me to a location for a filmed insert, although there was nothing for me to do other than to socialise and get to know the cast. This was the episode where Duncan wins a car at the Scouts summer fair, but Dudley forgets to post the insurance premium against someone winning it, and so Duncan forfeits his dream win. I guess the plot came from the old chestnut about someone forgetting to post the football pools, but as they say there are only so many plots, it is the way you write them that counts. That's my story, and I'm sticking to it!

For my second episode, *Matter Over Mind*, which was directed by Michael Mills, I managed to persuade him to use Pat in the small part of a bank manager's secretary. After all, the sitcom's title was a nod to nepotism, and by now Pat and I were married and living in Walthamstow.

Towards the end of the year I wrote another episode called *Alien Friends*. This was my favourite episode, because Brian Cooke was in America, overseeing the US version and I had no script editor interference or added or deleted dialogue. It was 100 per cent my own work. There was only one gag I had to excise from my script and that was a mother-in-law joke which Pauline Yates objected to for some reason. When I pointed out to her that Les Dawson told countless jokes about his mother-in-law, she said the comedian and his gags left her cold. Oh well, I thought, it's only two lines. There was no sense in arguing over one measly joke, so I agreed to cut it. And having seen *Guys and Dolls* at the National Theatre, I was delighted that David Healy, an American who played Nicely-Nicely Johnson in that production, was cast in my episode, and he was one of the nicest actors I had met in many years.

Repeat Performances

L ittle did I think when I first appeared in *Please Sir!* in 1968 that it would give us a healthy income when they repeated it in 1983. Because of the Equity agreements where terrestrial television was concerned, it meant that I was getting around £300 per episode, a huge difference between later royalties for satellite television, where you receive perhaps £300 for an entire series.

Back in 1983 though, that money was a lifesaver. While we still lived in Walthamstow, our daughter Emma was born. We bought a flat in Tunbridge Wells, and I managed the deposit from the money earned from the three episodes I wrote for *Keep It In The Family,* so the *Please Sir!* repeat money helped to pay the mortgage for a while, especially as the interest rates were climbing steadily and almost reached a staggering fifteen per cent.

Because many of us in *Please Sir!* had remained friends, and Richard Davies and his wife Jill lived not far away in Forest Hill, and Peter Cleall lived in Brighton, Pat and I formed a small-scale touring company, intending to tour *Under Milk Wood* with them to community and arts centres, mainly in the south east. We applied to the Enterprise Allowance Scheme, which gave us an income of £40 each for a year, no matter how much more money we might earn during that time. It was clearly a government scheme to adjust and lower the unemployment figures.

The idea for this production came about because I had been in two pantomimes at the Gatehouse Theatre in Stafford for two consecutive years while we still lived in Walthamstow. The second pantomime was *Aladdin*, with Valentine Dyall as Abanazer. I happened to be having a drink in the theatre bar with the Entertainments Manager, Philip Brewin, and I discovered he loved Dylan Thomas's play. He offered me a guarantee of £2,000 if I would produce it for three nights at his theatre a year later, with six actors. And so in 1982 we began to put the production together, with Dickie and Jill, Peter, Pat and myself. We still needed one other actor, and we managed to recruit

Peter Childs, who was a semi-regular actor in the popular *Minder* series for Euston Films.

I first met Peter in Cardiff in 1977, when we both appeared in *The Boys in The Band.* Also in the play was Barry Howard, whose mother lived in Nottingham, where Robin Stewart had a year earlier been visited by the police in his dressing room, telling us he had been assaulted by a club doorman. Barry, while visiting his mother in Nottingham, discovered Robin appeared in court as the accused and the plaintiff was the doorman, and we knew we had been right to treat Robin's story as just more of his bullshit.

Following a short tour of *The Boys in The Band,* Peter Childs and I became friends and throughout the late seventies I often visited him at his home in Tunbridge Wells. And it was Peter who suggested, when Pat and I were looking to buy a flat, that we try Tunbridge Wells, as we might get more for our money in Kent, rather than staying in London.

Although Peter occasionally appeared in *Minder*, playing DS Rycott, I hadn't expected him to show interest in our production which needed at least two weeks' solid rehearsal, followed by just three performances at Stafford. But he loved the play and the language, and launched himself into the roles of Mog Edwards, Cherry Owen and Mr Waldo with enthusiasm. If Peter was keen to do something, he gave himself to it one-hundred per cent. But if he didn't want to do something…

He told me that in 1979 LWT planned to do a series based on the old radio drama *Dick Barton, Special Agent.* The director, Jon Scoffield, asked to see Peter for the part of Snowy, Barton's sidekick. Peter traipsed up to London for the meeting, and Scoffield asked him how fit he was, and would he mind going into a gym for six weeks' training prior to the production. When Peter asked why, he was told there were fights and action sequences in every episode, and he needed to be in tip-top condition. Peter then asked the director how they planned on paying the actors for the time spent in training. Apparently, Scoffield hadn't thought this far ahead. Peter went on to say in a deliberately patronizing tone, 'You see, normally when actors do fight scenes they *act* them out. It's called *acting.* They don't *really* fight each other. They are *actors,* you see.'

When Peter told me this story, he said, 'I knew I was talking myself out of a job, but I'd already made up my mind I couldn't work for this director. He was a twat!'

Unfortunately for our *Milk Wood* production, after the three performances in Stafford Peter was committed to doing another two episodes of *Minder* and we had to replace him with Patrick Moore, an actor Pat and I had worked with in the Lionel Bart musical. We continued to tour to small venues, and I was staggered by just how popular Thomas's play was. At Trinity Theatre in Tunbridge Wells we were sold out three weeks prior to opening at this brand new arts centre in a converted church, and at most of the small venues and community centres they had to bring in extra seating.

It was during a break in our small-scale tour that I was offered a bilingual role. Made for television in 1983, *Owain Glendower, Prince of Wales* was shot back to back, a Welsh language version for showing on S4C and an English version for Channel 4. Both channels were less than a year old. The production company who made this film was English, as was the director, James Hill, and the brief they were given by S4C was that they must cast bilingual actors who had never appeared in the Welsh BBC soap, *Pobl y Cwm*. I had never been in the programme, and as I speak a little bit of Welsh, my agent suggested me to the casting director who was based in London. As they found it difficult to cast smaller roles in this production, I was accepted for the role of Second Soldier purely on the recommendation of my agent.

When the two bulky scripts dropped on to our doormat a few days later, I immediately read the English version with interest. I had often thought this great Welsh hero was a good subject for an exciting historical drama. But this wasn't it. As I turned the pages, mouth agape, I became more and more disappointed. Whoever had written this seemed to be attempting a family adventure along the lines of the old '50s and '60s series like *Ivanhoe*, *William Tell* and *Robin Hood*. There was even a corny scene straight out of a John Wayne western, where Owain exits a castle on horseback, along with his sidekick Rhodri, who spots one of Henry IV's snipers up a tree, about to kill Owain with an arrow. Rhodri fires one from the hip and fells the sniping archer, whereupon our hero salutes Rhodri and thanks him. 'Diolch, Rhodri!' And how do you do a John Wayne drawl in Welsh?

Halfway through reading the script, I gave up, only reading the scenes in which I was involved. A week later I caught the Holyhead train from Euston station, having been instructed to get off at Llandudno Junction, where a unit car would meet me to transport me to my hotel ready for filming the next day. It was there I met Martin Gower, the actor playing the First Soldier. Our characters seemed to be the comedy relief, a sort of double-act of two inept soldiers who end up being pushed into the river by Owain and his merry men in this travesty of a historical epic.

During the drive along the beautiful Conwy Valley we got to know each other, and I discovered that Martin's upbringing was similar to my own, having moved to England when he was young, with a Welsh tongue that was terribly rusty. But we thought we could cope with our six lines each, especially if we helped each other out in the hotel that evening.

Most of the cast and crew stayed in hotels in Betws-y-Coed, but Martin and I were quartered in a beautiful country manor hotel at Dolwyddelan, about four miles from Betws. As it was unusually perfect weather, we became rain cover. Most of our scenes were interiors, so we were kept on stand-by in case it should rain. It meant that in those pre mobile phone days we couldn't leave the hotel and had to hang around all day, eating and drinking. It was such a hardship tucking into freshly caught salmon, hooked in the nearby salmon leap by a waiter.

When they eventually decided to use us in a scene, we were picked up by 'Mr Jones the Taxi' who ferried many of the cast about. As we headed for the production office in Llanrwst, where make-up and wardrobe were based, Mr Jones told us he had been involved in many films, most notably *The Inn of The Sixth Happiness* which was shot in the Snowdonia region where they built an entire Chinese village on the mountainside near Beddgelert. Mr Jones reminisced about the halcyon days of chauffeuring Ingrid Bergman around Snowdonia when films were films, and they were well organised. 'Not like this lot,' he opined. 'This lot don't seem to know what they are doing.'

And to prove him right, when we got to Llanrwst one of the runners gabbled into his walkie-talkie about lost portable toilets which should have been on their way to the current location but were now heading in the wrong direction, leaving loads of actors and crew clutching the cheeks of their backsides tightly.

When I was kitted out in my chain-mail I went to make-up, to be reminded of the fact that I had been cast because I fitted the brief – no *Pobl y Cwm* appearances and a smattering of Welsh. But I was supposed to be a tough soldier, one of Henry IV's mercenaries, about to rape a fair maiden until rescued by Owain. The make-up woman stared at my face with concentration and declared, 'You look like Noddy. How am I going to make you look tough?'

I suggested a scar, but in my balaclava-like helmet there wasn't much room for a scar, and so I continued to look cute.

When we were ready, a unit car drove us to the location, the impressive Gwydir Castle, a fifteenth century fortified manor house less than two miles from Llanrwst. As the film had at least been blessed by sunny weather, exteriors were being filmed in the courtyard of the castle.

As soon as Martin and I arrived on the set we became acquainted with some of the other actors, and noticed a strange atmosphere, almost as if the cast were method actors and resented the English production company and crew. We soon discovered the reason for this when we were told by one of the actors that when he approached the director prior to shooting the Welsh version of a scene, asking if he could change a few lines as they were real tongue-twisters, the director said rather dismissively that he wasn't bothered about the Welsh version and could they just get on with it. Of course, word of this spread like wildfire throughout the cast, creating a lot of resentment. And the actors had now rechristened the production company 'Mickey Llygoden Films.'

When the director heard this, and asked what it meant, he wasn't pleased when he heard Llygoden meant 'mouse.'

Also staying at our hotel up in the hills was Dafydd, the location caterer, with whom we drank in the evenings, which explained our preferential treatment on the set at lunchtimes when we were offered a surreptitious 'livener' in our orange juice.

Dafydd had an assistant, Tom, who helped with the cooking. One morning I noticed Dafydd struggling on his own. I asked him what had happened to Tom. Looking over his shoulder and lowering his voice, Dafydd replied, 'Tom had to go back to Caernarfon to sign on.'

Outside our hotel was a small railway station, a request stop. The railway ran from Blaenau Ffestiniog via Betws-y-Coed to Llandudno Junction, and one night the three of us decided to go to Betws-y-Coed by train and drink with some of the other actors and crew at their hotel.

Just before midnight, when it looked as if the bar was closing, I had Mr Jones the Taxi's telephone number, but when I rang there was no reply. As it was pub turning-out time, I thought he might have been busy, but when I returned to the bar and told the barman there was no reply from his phone, he looked at his watch and said, 'Oh, you won't get Mr Jones now. He takes tablets.'

As we began to stagger back the four miles to our hotel, we hadn't gone very far when we spotted another hotel bar at the end of the main street, the lights still blazing and a certain amount of activity within. Fortified and optimistic after our boozing session, we entered to find the hotel manager busy clearing up. When we explained our predicament to him, he said he lived just beyond Dolwyddelan and offered us a lift back. Not only that, he sold us a round of drinks while he finished clearing up.

The following day, feeling a bit jaded, as soon as lunchtime came around, Dafydd stuck another 'livener' in our orange juice.

I never did see the end result of this film and my tough soldier performance. But a friend saw it, and I was told I looked rather sweet.

Usually, when actors work in a large budget, made-for-television film, over the years they receive small cheques for repeats or sales from abroad. I don't think I ever received a residual cheque for the Owain Glyndŵr film, so presumably and deservedly it sank without trace.

Commercial Break

Perhaps because of the *Please Sir!* repeats in 1983, Malcolm and I were offered a Sealink commercial, he as a prospective bridegroom heading for a wedding in Belgium, with me as his best man. He was the driver going onto the ferry, and I was his passenger. During the crossing, the client, a man from Sealink, said they had made several commercials and one of the actors mentioned publicly how bad the food was on the Sealink ships. For our night in Ostend, the Sealink man promised, provided we kept quiet about the ship's grub, by way of thanks we would be treated to a sumptuous meal at an expensive seafood restaurant and could order what we liked.

By way of thanks or a bribe we wondered?

But the final shot of the day was of Malcolm and his bride waving from the dock, with me waving back from the last ship that evening heading for Dover. In case shooting wasn't complete in Belgium, they got me a double, and planned sending him back on the ship instead. Otherwise it would be me eating Sealink food instead of lobster thermidor.

There had to be some way of keeping me in Belgium for the night. It was Malcolm who came up with an idea.

For one of the shots, the director wanted him to drive us round a roundabout and up a slip road leading onto a motorway. He instructed us to drive to the next turn-off and then head back to the roundabout, where the runner would be waiting to direct us to the church for the wedding scene, a montage of still photographs.

As we reached the turn-off, instead of heading back down the motorway, Malcolm drove us into the countryside, where we found a small pub. We went inside, ordered two beers and played a couple of rock 'n' roll numbers on the juke box. Half an hour later we headed back to the roundabout where we found the runner waiting patiently. We told him we had missed the first turn-off and had to go on to the next.

When we arrived at the church, we discovered Malcolm's bride was played by Koo Stark, an American actress, model and photographer who was in a relationship with Prince Andrew for a time.

The church sequence of wedding photographs took little time, and despite Malcolm's helpful attempts to waste time for my benefit, I managed to catch that last ship home. The director warned that the last shot of me waving from the ferry was important and said he would keep the camera rolling. I had to keep on waving for as long as possible as it was on a long zoom.

Days later Malcolm told me what had happened. As the ship distanced itself from the harbour, the crew said it was a wrap, and one of them chuckled and said, 'Look, the tosser's still waving. I wonder how long he'll keep that up.'

I continued waving until I could barely see Belgium, and other people on the deck probably thought I was mad.

I was mad. Mad I had to eat Sealink chow as I imagined the film crew tucking into fresh lobster.

Friends From *Please Sir!*

In 1984 Richard Davies became a regular character in *The Bottle Boys*, a television comedy about milkmen, with Robin Askwith as the leading bottle boy. Around the same time I was offered one episode of *Brookside* as a Buildings Enforcement Officer. At the read-through, before reading the script, the director, Eszter Nordin, handed out books of poetry to read by way of a warm-up. Afterwards I asked one of the regular actors in the series was this usually the way they began their read-throughs, and I was told it had never happened before and she was a new director.

I hung around Liverpool, mainly the pubs, because I couldn't believe how much cheaper alcohol was compared to the south east. They didn't get to my scene for a good four or five days, a storyline where one of the main characters puts up an extension on his house without planning permission, and I was the baddie from the council giving him grief. My parting shot was, 'You haven't heard the last of this.'

But it was the last he heard of it because as a storyline it was a damp squib and they didn't follow it up. When I watched the episode, the riveting tag before the commercial break was someone's quiche getting burnt in the oven. Electrifying.

It was in 1984 that I heard about the death of Noel Howlett, our brilliant and well-loved incompetent Fenn Street headmaster, which I always thought was perfect casting for Noel. He played it brilliantly. And he did work again in another Esmonde and Larbey sitcom which I remember well, *The Good Life,* and also appeared in an episode of *Sykes*, which of course Deryck Guyler was also in, playing PC Corker Turnbull, which was a regular character for Deryck.

1985 was to be an eventful year. Our son, Morgan was born on 21 April. We played some more *Under Milk Wood* dates, but as they were embarking on a second series of *Bottle Boys*, it meant Richard Davies wouldn't be available. We performed at the Stag Theatre, Sevenoaks, and Peter Cleall suggested

Brian Hall could take over as Captain Cat, so he brought him along to watch the performance.

Brian was the amiable chef in *Fawlty Towers*, and I had worked with him in a television commercial for Glengettie Tea, showing only in Wales. The scene was a wedding reception, Brian was the bridegroom and I was best man. Although we made speeches, the ad was mute, and they played a jingle or a song over the action. What happened was our speeches became outrageously ribald, with the director falling about and encouraging us. The dialogue became so blue with each of us trying to top each other, seeing how far we could go in Derek and Clive filth, that some of the other wedding guests choked on their tea and had to spit it out. But the director loved it. When I told someone about this later on, they pointed out that if any deaf people watched the commercial, they would have great fun lip reading our speeches.

Brian, like many actors attracted to the Welsh play with its wonderful imagery, gave Captain Cat an exemplary interpretation. Unlike Alan Leith, who took over from me when I agreed to appear in an episode of *Bottle Boys*.

Leo Dolan was a regular in the first series of the milkmen sitcom, but when offered an episode in the second series I heard that he said he wanted 'nothing more to do with that crap.' I was interviewed by director Stuart Allen for the part and was offered too much money to turn it down. It clashed with a week at the Pomegranate Theatre at Chesterfield for *Milk Wood* where we were offered a £2,000 guarantee, and apart from paying six actors and a stage manager, the costs incurred in the running of the production were negligible.

Alan Leith was a Brighton-based actor, who had appeared in the original production of *Blood Brothers* with Barbara Dickson. On Peter Cleall's recommendation I cast him as First Voice, taking over from me in Thomas's play at Chesterfield, while I performed in an episode of *Bottle Boys*.

When we first produced this version of *Milk Wood* in 1983, I realized the only way to learn the lines was by memorising at least two or three speeches every night for three weeks prior to the start of rehearsals. I mentioned this to Alan Leith many weeks before we began, telling him it was the only way to learn the First Voice. When he turned up on the first day of rehearsal with the script in his hand, and clearly hadn't learnt a single line, I was surprised and annoyed. I had directed this as Dylan Thomas had intended, using two voices instead of one narrator, and Peter Cleall was the Second Voice. It looked most odd that Peter knew the lines, but Leith as First Voice performed with a book in his hand. But there was nothing I could do about it. Either the actor hadn't attempted to learn the lines, or he had tried and failed. I just had to accept it.

Following my unremarkable, nothing-to-write-home-about performance in *Bottle Boys*, which I think was recorded on a Monday night, I set off for Chesterfield late on Tuesday night, with Emma fast asleep in the back of the car, then joined Pat at the digs she'd found. I didn't see Alan Leith, who played the Tuesday performance then high-tailed it back to Brighton, knowing I was coming to take over for the rest of the week. Everyone in the cast was getting £285.00, which in today's money is worth over £800.00. Alan got his payment before he left for home, so that wasn't bad money for just two performances and reading from a script.

I played the rest of the week for nothing, but at least Pat was on an equal share like everyone else.

The following year I played Norman, a bar manager, in *Never the Twain*. I enjoyed working with Windsor Davies and Donald Sinden. During a camera rehearsal break, I went with Windsor to the Anglers pub, a handy retreat next door to Teddington Studios. Usually, if someone recognises you in a pub they want to buy you a drink. Not Windsor. It was the other way round. He would buy the whole pub a drink. I've never known anyone so generous.

And Donald Sinden was a very giving actor, whispering to me in the camera rehearsal which camera favoured me the most, secretly telling me I wouldn't get that advice from the director, Robert Reed.

John Howard Davies, who used to be Head of Comedy at BBC Television, was now a producer at Thames TV. He started out as a child actor and played Oliver Twist in the David Lean film with Alec Guinness as Fagin. He cast me as Arthur in *We'll Think of Something*, written by Geoff Rowley who co-wrote some of *Fenn Street*'s first series.

To be honest, I can't really remember much of what this series was about. It starred Sam Kelly and it wasn't recommissioned. But I do remember meeting Robin Hayter who was in it and talking to him about how supportive his father James Hayter was when he said he would have liked to 'kick that cunt' Dave King down the stairs for me. Robin laughed and said, 'Yeah, that sounds like Dad!'

Because we had done so well with our small-scale tour of *Under Milk Wood*, and the only props we toured were six bentwood chairs, I wanted to produce another production, benefiting from the goodwill of the theatres we had played, but I couldn't think of anything that didn't involve scenery, which would then mean transporting a set and all the paraphernalia that went with it. And then it struck me! Radio has no scenery. I thought I could produce a comedy radio show, standing around a BBC microphone as if it was a live recording. I had a word with Dickie, Jill, Peter Cleall, Patrick Moore, and of course Pat, and everyone thought it was a good idea. I called it *Radio Fun* and put together an idea for a show kicking off with *ITMA* in the War Years, with The Glums from *Take It from Here, The Goon Show, Hancock's Half Hour* and *Round the Horne*.

First though, I needed to get theatre touring rights and my first contact was BBC Enterprises, who demanded six per cent of the box office. When I contacted Norma Farnes, Spike Milligan's agent and friend for more than thirty-five years, she was extremely helpful. When I told her what the BBC wanted percentage wise, she told me Spike owned the copyright to his *Goon Show* scripts, and she told me to tell the BBC to fuck off.

For years after our conversation I had this fantasy of me dialling the BBC switchboard and telling them to fuck off.

Norma went on to suggest I offer them one per cent just for the goodwill. She also gave me the names of the other writers' agents and how to contact them.

When I contacted Barry Took about *Round the Horne*, he said I could use the rights for free, he didn't want any money, and said he could also speak on behalf of Mary Feldman, even without the aid of Doris Stokes.[3]

The show began its small-scale tour in 1987. I wrote additional material linking each episode, which the rest of the cast narrated in a documentary style, all of us standing around an old-fashioned BBC coffin-shaped microphone, and used props for the sound effects, which added a visual mood to each episode. Apart from *ITMA*, where we made a few cuts because the humour was so dated, every episode was as fresh as when it was first written, the audiences enjoyed it and the show received good reviews.

Following many one- and two-night stands of our radio theatre show, I was asked to direct the Sevenoaks Stag Theatre's first professional pantomime. I was offered a *Cinderella* script by Christopher Timothy, and I asked Malcolm McFee if he would join me as a Broker's Man. Meanwhile, Maggie Durdant-Hollamby who ran the theatre, wanted a name to top the bill as Buttons. I had been watching *The Lenny Henry Show*, and I thought the young actor, Vas Blackwood, who played Winston in that show was rather good and very funny. We cast him, and on the first day of rehearsal at Sevenoaks, which I

---

3   Doris Stokes was a well-known psychic and clairvoyant.

called for 11.00 a.m. to allow the actors to get the cheaper fares, Blackwood didn't turn up until nearly 11.45, saying he'd left his wallet at home. Fair enough, I thought, that was just bad luck. But he was late most days, and often he didn't even bother to make excuses. Because I called rehearsals for eleven, I expected everyone to work until six – at least. Not Blackwood, who left dead on half-five, saying, 'I've got a train to catch, man.'

To say I regretted casting him is an understatement, but the buck stopped with me.

I've been in some technical rehearsals in productions which go on until late at night. This particular one, with Malcolm's help, was reasonably smooth and we were well into the second half by six o'clock with only another hour to go. But Vas Blackwood said he was going. Walking out. The stage manager went ape, screaming at him and swearing, and in the end a cowed Buttons stayed until we finished the tech. But Malcom and I wanted Blackwood to walk out, because then we could have sacked him without pay, and got David Sargent, who played the Major Domo to take over the role, as he was so much better. But we were stuck with Vas Blackwood for the entire run. And I can remember Malcolm whispering to me in the wings, as he watched Blackwood's performance as Buttons, 'You'd think some of Lenny Henry's professionalism would have rubbed off on the bloke, wouldn't you?'

When I saw him in Guy Ritchie's *Lock, Stock and Two Smoking Barrels* some years later, I wondered if he was still annoyingly uncooperative.

The following year we played a few more dates with *Radio Fun*. Over a drink following a performance, I can remember Dickie telling us a funny story. When he was a young actor he auditioned at a West End theatre for an American musical. He finished performing his song and there was a hiatus. So he stepped forward and, while peering into the blackness of the auditorium, asked, 'Are you looking for actors who can sing or singers who can act?'

An American voice flew at him from the darkness of the stalls, 'In your case, buddy – neither!'

Mostly, we performed one-night stands of *Radio Fun*, which meant that word-of-mouth and good reviews could do us no good whatsoever. Then, for two weeks in the autumn, we were offered a weekly guarantee of £1,750 to take our show to the Theatre Royal, Margate.

Patrick Moore had to drop out of the production, due to another commitment, and Arthur White took his place. Arthur, David Jason's brother, went on to play PC Ernie Trigg in *A Touch of Frost*. When I first met Arthur,

141

I'm not sure if he wore a medallion or not, but he did wear some sort of metal bracelet, a rather snazzy gold watch, and his car had a go-faster-stripe along it. I was tickled to think he may have helped model his brother's 'Del boy' character. But Arthur was a lovely bloke to work with and very professional.

The theatre belonged to Jolyon Jackley, the son of the late comic actor Nat Jackley. Jolyon Jackley followed in his father's footsteps for a time, and when he was merely a babe in arms he appeared briefly as Ann Todd's son in the David Lean film *The Sound Barrier*.

Margate Theatre Royal was built during the reign of George III, making it the second oldest English provincial theatre. The interior was restored by J. T. Robinson, who designed the Old Vic, and the Margate theatre, with its horseshoe-shaped design, is a miniature version of the London theatre. After surviving nearly 200 years as a playhouse, it became a cinema in the 1950s, followed by a stint as a bingo hall before falling into neglect and abandonment. Then rescue came when Jolyon Jackley purchased the leasehold of the listed building and restored it to its former splendour.

The theatre is tucked on the side of a hill at the end of a quiet Georgian square. Sitting in the auditorium you felt good, it was cosy and intimate, and we felt as though we had been shrunk to fit in one of those Victorian toy theatres.

Our Margate *Radio Fun* week opened on a Monday night, and because the theatre had a cheaper ticket offer for opening nights, we were off to a great start. It was one of the friendliest theatres I have ever worked in. At the end of each performance, we met in the Circle Bar, where everyone got to know everyone – performers, theatre staff and those of the audience who stayed for a drink.

On our second Friday into the run, we promised Emma (seven-years-old now) that she could watch the performance. We were worried about leaving her in the audience by herself while we were on stage, and so we asked Yvonne, one of the usherettes, to keep an eye on her. We were not long into the first act when we saw Emma leave her seat and creep away. Pat and I found it difficult to concentrate until she returned to her seat five minutes later. After the performance I asked Emma if she had popped out to go to the loo. She replied, 'Oh, no. I went to see Yvonne about my ice cream for the interval.'

During our first week of performances at this 500 seat theatre we played to about fifty per cent, but the second week built to around eighty per cent, and the box office took more than the guaranteed sum they were paying us.

THEATRE ROYAL
MARGATE

Built 1786

Reopened 1988

Box Office Thanet (0843) 221913

From Monday, 18th September to Saturday, 30th September
For Two Weeks Only
Mon — Sat Eves 8.00pm   Matinée Thursdays 3.00pm

'NOT THE BBC'
presents

RICHARD DAVIES   PETER CLEALL
DAVID BARRY
PAT CARLILE   JILL BRITTON
IN

RADIO FUN

THE GOLDEN YEARS OF RADIO COMEDY
LIVE ON STAGE!

Scripts by: **TED KAVANAGH, SPIKE MILLIGAN,**
FRANK MUIR & DENIS NORDEN, RAY GALTON
& ALAN SIMPSON and BARRY TOOK &
MARTY FELDMAN

OAP's Children & Party Rates Available
Saver Performances Mon Eves & Thurs Matinées

Apart from this brighter episode towards the end of the decade, I was devastated by the loss of my friend Peter Childs who died at the age of 50 from leukaemia. I went to see him at his cottage in Hawkhurst just four weeks before the end, and despite his shrunken, hollow appearance as he lay in his bed, he still had a cheeky smile as he laughed and joked, his eyes sparkling with each witticism. I often catch repeats of his *Minder* episodes, and I am always staggered by how good he was. Like Brian Hall, Peter enjoyed making up rhyming slang, and as he suffered from piles, he referred to the disorder as his Chalfonts – as in Chalfonts St Giles. One night I watched an episode of *Minder* which Peter wasn't in, and Arthur Daley said to Terry McCann, 'My Chalfonts ain't half playing up, Terry.' I wondered if Peter had been drinking with one of the *Minder* writers.

Peter's Chalfonts got so bad at one stage, he had to go into hospital for an operation to have them cut out. Afterwards he told me it was horrendous because halfway through the op the anaesthetic wore off, and he said he was screaming with pain. And then he added, with that twinkle in his eye, 'Mind you, I know how I could play Edward the Second now.'

Earlier in the decade I made a Christmas commercial for Harveys Bristol Cream Sherry, shot in a hospital ward set where all the patients were in traction, passing the drink around on a pulley. I lay in bed next to Michael Elwyn. I had no idea at the time that he was a close friend of Peter Childs. When I attended Peter's memorial service at the Actors' Church in Covent Garden, Michael Elwyn paid a tribute to him with a funny story about a time when they toured together.

They shared the journey to each venue in one car. Michael was a keen golfer and had an expensive set of golf clubs on the back seat of the car. Peter had a plastic supermarket bag containing his theatre make-up and shaving tackle. The car was broken into, and the thief stole Peter's flimsy bag of make-up but left the golf clubs behind. They informed the police about the break-in and later that day a young constable was sent to interview them at the theatre.

'Have you any idea who might have stolen this item?' the constable asked Peter.

'Well, constable,' Peter replied, 'I suggest you scour the town and search for a clean-shaven, non-golfing tramp, wearing Number Five Eye-liner.'

***

If someone in the acting profession died, I don't know why but it was often Peter Cleall who heard it first and shared the news This he did in 1992 when Joan Sanderson passed-away. Since *Please Sir!* she had probably been one of the busiest of the ex-Fenn Street School actors, appearing in many sitcoms, and I loved watching her in *Me And My Girl,* with my old mate Richard O'Sullivan as a widower struggling to bring up a teenage daughter, with Joan as his rather formidable mother-in-law, but deep down a rather sympathetic and understanding person. But the one television role she did that I treasure the most since playing Fenn Street's Miss Ewell was the episode she did of *Fawlty Towers,* in which she played an unforgiving battle axe hotel guest with hearing aid issues. I have seen it so many times (haven't we all?) and I still enjoy her interaction with John Cleese. It was typical of Joan, perfectly studied. Brilliant!

Peter was one of the founder members of Pelham Associates, a cooperative actors' agency. I applied to join and, after being accepted as a member, like all the other actors at the agency my commitment was in working as an agent in the Brighton office for one day a week, which later changed to fortnightly as the membership increased. Apart from Peter, I was the only other actor from *Please Sir!* to be represented by Pelham Associates.

One of my first interviews when I joined Pelham in 1995 was for *A Mind to Kill,* a crime series starring Philip Madoc as DCI Noel Bain. The actor is probably most remembered for playing the infamous U-boat captain in *Dad's Army.* Peter Edwards was the director, who was interested in me playing a character in an episode titled *Rachel Hardcastle,* featuring Siân Phillips. As the production was shot in both Welsh and English, I hoped the character didn't have too many lines. When I met Peter Edwards, he was very persuasive, telling me I would have no problem with the part. I guessed, because he was Meredith Edwards's son, with whom I had toured in *Milk Wood,* and he had seen my work, he was keen to offer me the role.

I played a henpecked husband, whose hobby was making model cars,. In my first scene, which was shot in a council house in Penarth, near Cardiff, I met Gillian Griffiths, who played my wife, and it was later pointed out to me that she was the mother of Ioan Gruffudd, who I always admired as Horatio Hornblower in the ITV series *Hornblower.*

As I struggled to solder one of my toy cars in the scene (echoes of Frankie Abbott here), she belittled me, and I ended up shoving the soldering iron into her throat, although the police technical adviser on the series told us the wound would be cauterized by the tool, and so I finished her off by strangling her.

One of the actors I got talking to during breaks from filming was Michael Povey, a regular in the series as Superintendent Jack Bevan, having been promoted from when he was Detective Constable Jones in *Minder*. I asked him which actor he preferred working with, Patrick Malahide or Peter Childs. Unhesitatingly he replied Peter as Rycott. And when I asked him why, I had rightly guessed it was because he enjoyed Peter's company and sense of humour.

The murder scene, and the subsequent arrival of the police and crime scene investigation took two or three days to film. Everything takes longer in back-to-back shoots as each scene is shot in both languages. I had a break of two weeks until my next scene in the police interview room on location at Newport, being interrogated by DCI Bain. I had more dialogue in this scene and I was worried about the Welsh version. But by the time my train from Paddington arrived at Newport, I thought I could have performed the scene in my sleep. When I got to the location, I was introduced to Philip Madoc, and then it was straight into a brief rehearsal of the scene, beginning with my confession. Philip Madoc looked totally blank, and I thought my Welsh must have been abysmal. Then Peter Edwards stepped in and said, 'Which script are you working from?' I told him it was the one I had been sent six weeks ago. He then told me it had been rewritten and nobody had thought to send me a copy of the new script. He must have seen the panic in my eyes because he told everyone to take a fifteen minute break, then took me into an office, and patiently directed me through each word of the new dialogue. We returned to shoot the scene, and the Welsh version we got in two takes. I must have relaxed after that, because when we came to shoot the English version, I dried.

In 1981 Pat and I had appeared in *Captain Stirrick* for the Children's Film Unit, run by director and writer Colin Finbow, a British film production unit which offered children from the ages of 10 to 16 a chance to learn about all aspects of filmmaking, participating as part of the crew in the making of professional-quality feature films, or performing. And they used professional actors in the adult roles. The films had a theatrical release, as well as being shown on British and overseas television, and were exhibited at international film festivals.

In 1996, Colin Finbow offered me a small part as a milkman in *The Gingerbread House* for the CFU. When I arrived at the location I saw how worried the director was because the film ratio had taken it way over budget because one of the younger child actors had needed six takes in a scene. Developing celluloid film is costly, so the less footage that is shot the lower the cost of production. I asked Colin what his ratio was, and he told me it was 3:1. In the CFU a foot of every three feet of film shot had to end up on the screen. Normal ratio for a Hollywood film would be about 10:1 – in other words, a 90 minute feature film would shoot roughly 25 hours of film. And the rest!

I suggested to Colin that we rehearse my scene with the kids three or four times before attempting a take, then hopefully we could get the ratio back on track. We managed the scene with just one take, and Colin was delighted to get his ratio back to 3:1.

We had a holiday in Llanberis that year and managed to climb Snowdon. The great thing about the long trek to the summit is the bar and café at the peak, which rewards you with a pint or two. But on a clear day, like the one we had, it's worth the climb for the view alone.

We hadn't long returned from our holiday when we received news that Liz Gebhardt had died. I had known for many years she had cancer, but it was still a sad day with my friend gone. I remembered all the silly times we had, like a lot of us walking along Wardour Street to a screening when we spotted John Cleese on the other side of the road. And because watching *Monty Python's Flying Circus* was all the rage then, and we had enjoyed episodes with the hedgehogs Spiny Norman and Dinsdale, Liz and all of us yelled across the street at Cleese, 'Dinsdale! Dinsdale!' He rightly ignored it and carried on walking, fairly normally I seem to recall.

But that was my great friend Liz, who was always up for a laugh.

Liz had been with her family on her deathbed and said her goodbyes. She told Ian she didn't want grieving; she wanted everyone to really go to town and celebrate her life. So, after the funeral, in their back garden Ian had hired caterers and opened bottles of champagne, and she had dozens of mourners all partying to celebrate her life.

***

Although I had donned drag to play Ugly Sister in *Cinderella* at Oxford, in 1996 I was offered my first dame role in *Babes in The Wood* at Leeds City Varieties. The writer and director was Robin Davies, the actor who was Carrot, the young boy in *Catweazle*. I got on really well with Robin, and discovered he was from Tywyn in North Wales. We occasionally exchanged words or sentences in Welsh, but Robin was fluent, whereas I could only manage short phrases. He told me his real name was Richard Davies but Equity wouldn't allow two members of the same name, and so he adopted the name 'Robin'.

I arrived in Leeds on Sunday night and checked into my theatre digs. Villa Novello was an enormous house owned by Basil Hartley. When I had telephoned to book a room, he told me he would charge fifty pounds for the week, or I could have the luxury one Danny La Rue always had at sixty pounds. I chose Danny's room. As Basil welcomed me after my long drive, he offered me a cup of coffee and showed me into his kitchen. He gestured to a cosy chair by the fire, saying, 'Sit there. That's Danny's chair.'

Any performers who have ever worked City Varieties will know how small it used to be backstage, and if you exited stage right, you were stuck there until the next scene, as there was no room to cross at the back. So I asked Robin if I could always exit left. Not that I needed to do any quick changes. They provided only two dame costumes for this production, one for the first half and one for the second. I should have kicked up a fuss, and demanded more costumes, especially as it is traditional for dames to have different novelty costumes for each scene, so they can get a laugh on every entrance. But I stifled my complaints because I liked Robin Davies and I really didn't want to upset him.

Robin Hood in the production was played by Brad Clayton, who was Chris 'Skippy' Newman in *London's Burning,* and Joanne Heywood, Dilys from *First of the Summer Wine,* was his Maid Marian. They both had a love duet before the finale, but prior to that Robin had devised a battle between the Sheriff of Nottingham, King John and the audience. The two baddies fired cheap, black-painted footballs from a cannon at the audience, and the audience retaliated, having been armed by the young dancers with sponges that looked like rocks. Mayhem ensued as these missiles were wildly exchanged to Valkyries music and much dry ice. But unlike the Christmas show at West Yorkshire Playhouse, which attracted the more genteel children, our City Varieties kids were rougher and tougher, and some of the more astute little brats saved their rock/sponges until the love duet when it caused more hilarity to pelt Robin and Marian in mid song.

I made the mistake of telling Morgan this before he, Emma and Pat came to see the show. That night Joanne was hit in the mouth just as she reached the final high note. Brad came off stage laughing as she said, 'Which little bastard threw that rock?'

Later, Morgan boasted that his aim had been brilliant.

Around this time, UK Gold repeated the *Please Sir!* series, followed by *The Fenn Street Gang*. There were twelve regular characters in the former, and six of us in the latter. So it surprised me when a cheque for *Fenn Street* repeats came to only around half of the school series. I telephoned the Artistes' Payments at Granada, the company who now owned the rights to the series and asked them why only half the money. Surely, I pointed out, as there were only six regular characters in *Fenn Street,* it should have been double the money. Then I was told that because the later series was less popular, Granada had leased it to Gold for less money.

Earlier in the decade I was invited to an event at Planet Hollywood to celebrate the book launch of Paul Gambaccini and Rod Taylor's *Television's Greatest Hits*. I was invited because two episodes in which I was heavily featured, *The Facts of Life* in *Please Sir!* and *The Thin Yellow Line* in *The Fenn Street Gang,* both reached number one in the ratings. I met Brian Murphy again, and spent some time chatting to him. He was invited because two of his *George and Mildred* episodes had also reached the top slots.

But a most fortuitous gift was a copy of the book we were all given. After I had telephoned Granada, I searched the book for the ratings figures and discovered *Please Sir!* spent 29 weeks in the ratings, whereas *Fenn Street* topped it at 31 weeks. And because Granada were hand in glove with Gold, it looked suspiciously like a sweetheart deal. Or as Equity liked to say, they didn't have an 'arm's length agreement.'

I got on to Equity and the Writers' Guild armed with proof of *Fenn Street*'s popularity, they got in touch with the TV company, an independent arbitrator was appointed, and much later cheques arrived in the post for both actors and writers involved in the *Fenn Street* series.

Nearly two years later, Bill Kenwright asked Peter at Pelham Associates if I would give him a ring. When I spoke to Bill, he offered me what would become my final No.1 Tour. It was a Ray Cooney farce called *Funny Money* and I was offered the part of the taxi driver. My billing on the poster mentioned *Fenn Street Gang* even though it had been 25 years since I appeared in it, but perhaps the reason Kenwright offered me the job was because of the 1996 repeats on UK Gold. In the show were Henry McGee, Trevor Bannister, Gareth Hunt, Deborah Watling, Anita Graham, and playing the lead was Rodney Bewes.

It was a good cast for the touring production. Henry McGee was very popular, and audiences loved him in *The Benny Hill Show;* Trevor Bannister

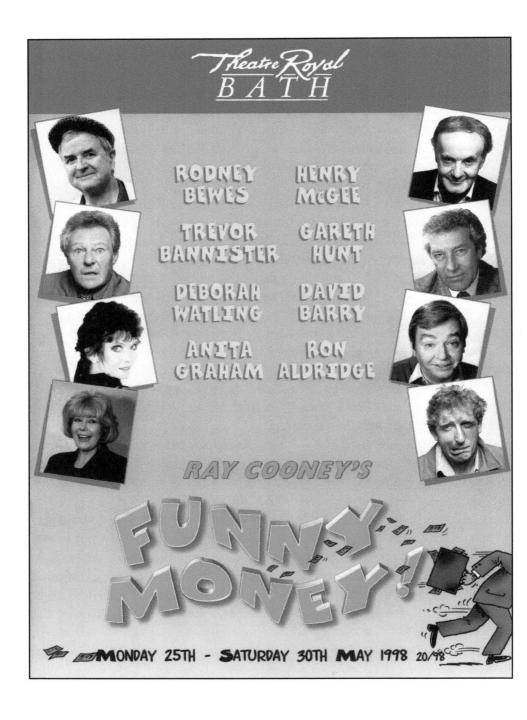

everyone remembered from *Are You Being Served?* He had a wealth of theatre experience and early in his career he played the title role of *Billy Liar* in the theatre, having taken over from Albert Finney. Gareth Hunt was very familiar to audiences for his role as Mike Gambit in *The New Avengers,* and Deborah Watling many still remembered as one of Dr Who's assistants. Anita Graham had been in dozens of plays, especially comedies, and played Tina in several series of *Terry and June.* She was also in the Sam Cree farce in Torquay with my wife Zélie in the early seventies when I drank with Charles Hawtrey, completely free of charge.

I had heard much about Rodney Bewes from many actors over the years, none of it good. And I recalled doing a voice over with Warren Clarke and James Bolam, years ago, around the time of *Whatever Happened to the Likely Lads.* The first thing Clarke said to Bolam was 'How's the beast?' And Bolam rolled his eyes and sighed, 'Still the same.'

Now I would find out what it was like working with Rodney Bewes. The opening night at Theatre Royal, Windsor was a near disaster. We were called for a cue-to-cue technical rehearsal as late as noon and, as I anticipated, we ran out of time and were unable to do entrances and exits in Act 2 as we had to do the dress rehearsal in the afternoon. That rehearsal was a shambles, with Rodney shutting the door on the set when it should have been left open and vice versa. And he seemed to be taking a prompt for every other line. Panic started to grip.

Sweating in the wings, prior to the performance, Gareth Hunt said he had never been so nervous. But the audience appeared not to notice the many cock-ups and laughed uproariously at everything. The second act, though, was abysmal, like wading through syrup. Rodney had lost it, and Trevor Bannister was doing his nut in the wings. Every time Rodney inadvertently shut the door when it should have been left open, Trevor hissed: 'Leave the fucking door, stupid cunt!'

In the dressing room after the show, Mark Piper, the artistic director of the theatre, came into the dressing room I shared with Ron Aldridge, the director, and I sensed an atmosphere. I decided to head quickly for the bar, but not before I heard Ron telling Mark Piper, 'We all make mistakes. I can accept that. But he's done a bottle of port in the interval, and that's something I find unforgivable.'

In the Stalls Bar, I sat beside Trevor, who ran Rodney down. And when Rodney appeared, sheepish and quiet, clutching a glass of Coca Cola, Trevor muttered, 'The cunt has the cheek to drink Coke. He's not fooling anybody.'

Ron called a line rehearsal for the next day, which was Press Night. Bill Kenwright wanted Rodney to continue, probably because he was popular and *Whatever Happened to the Likely Lads* was being repeated on BBC television.

Things marginally improved, maybe because Henry McGee took Rodney in hand. The curious thing about Rodney was the fact that had I not been the one to approach him and make polite conversation, he would have ignored me totally. It took me until almost the end of this twelve week tour to speculate why this was, and then I realized. It was maybe because he knew Liz Gebhardt had been a close friend of mine, and he guessed she might have told me about the time she played his girlfriend in the third series of *Dear Mother, Love Albert*, which he wrote. He spent a great deal of time trying to get Liz into bed, but she wasn't having any of it and rejected his advances, staying loyal to Ian. When it came to the fourth series, he insisted on recasting Cheryl Hall as his girlfriend instead of Liz. Of course, Bewes would have been armed with the excuse that during the first episode of his fourth series Liz was unavailable for that first episode, but as he was not only writer of his own series, he was also co-producer, and it wouldn't have taken him a great stretch of imagination to write her out of episode one and bring her into the second episode.

Years later, Liz told me she attended a function at the Savoy Hotel and Rodney was there. 'Hello, Liz,' he said brightly. And then she embarrassed him by saying loudly, 'Don't talk to me, you cunt!'

So, maybe Rodney guessed that I knew all about his behaviour, although I never did tell anyone else in the *Funny Money* cast, mainly because I hadn't given it much thought until the tour almost ended.

Escape Into Print

Not long after the *Funny Money* tour ended, Pat and I split up, and I moved into a flat in the village of Rusthall, on the outskirts of Tunbridge Wells. It was then I began to concentrate on writing, and I wrote *Each Man Kills*, both as a novel and a television script. Carlton TV optioned it, and I got excited thinking it would be turned into a series. Unfortunately, when Carlton offered it to ITV, the decision maker rejected it on the grounds that they were not keen on dramas set in Wales. I was astounded by that attitude, and so was Jonathan Powell, Carlton's Head of Drama, who then bought another option on my script and offered it to BBC Wales as a Carlton production. But it wasn't long before BBC Wales rejected it, saying they weren't looking for a police drama.

So that was that, but at least I found a publisher for the novel which was published in 2002.

When I was busy writing this police drama in 1999, I heard Deryck Guyler had died in Brisbane, Australia. He moved there with his wife Paddy when he retired, to be near his youngest son, daughter-in-law and the grandchildren. His death suddenly brought back forgotten memories of times spent in his company. Like the time he involved all us 5C actors in a charity event in south London, and afterwards we were taken back to his house in Norbury for tea, and then he entertained us by playing some jazz records while he played the washboard. And being asked to hide in the hospitality room with other guests at Thames Television's Euston Road studios so that Eamonn Andrews could spring a surprise on him with that red book.

The television shows he did after his Norman Potter roles were again with that wonderfully distinctive voice of his, especially when he appeared as P.C. Corky Turnbull in dozens of episodes of *Sykes*. But the last time I recall hearing his distinctive tones was as an animated skeleton for the Scotch Video Tapes commercials. And whenever I hear Bob Mortimer's voice of the bulldog in the Churchill Insurance ads, I can't help wondering if he deliberately modelled it on Deryck's characteristic delivery.

More recently I looked up Deryck on YouTube and was delighted to see him playing his washboard on *The Morcombe and Wise Show.*

I had known for some time that Malcolm McFee had cancer but didn't realize how bad it was until he phoned me up early in November 2001, telling me he was contracted to play Dame at the Elgiva Theatre, Chesham, in *Beauty and the Beast,* but felt too ill to cope. He asked me would I take over, and I agreed. This was only just over a week before rehearsals were due to commence on a Saturday at Chesham. Malcolm said he would still be co-directing the show, along with David Roden, the theatre manager, and he looked forward to seeing me on the following Saturday. But on Monday I received a phone call from his daughter Victoria, telling me her dad had passed-away and the funeral was on Friday.

The funeral was at Braintree in Essex, where Malcolm lived with his second wife Jacqui and their son Calum. Most funerals are sad events, but this one particularly so because Calum was only three-years-old, and it is doubtful he will ever remember anything about his father, other than unreliable memories when he sees DVDs of his father's TV performances as he gets older.

At the funeral I met director David Roden, who was employing me by default, and we both agreed it would be hard to get into the pantomime spirit the very next day.

Saturday morning in the theatre auditorium we were about to start with a read-through of the script. But before starting, David Roden, perhaps as an ice-breaker, had bought two boxes of wine, one red and one white, containing the equivalent of three bottles each, and told the cast to help themselves to a drink. It was bizarre, knocking back the booze at 10.30 in the morning when we were really there to work. *This has the makings of a disaster*, I remember thinking. And the script, written by Roden, was mediocre.

After the read-through we began blocking the first half of the show. Blocking is working out the moves, who stands where, and who enters and exits from which side of the stage etc. It is more of a technical start to the proceedings, rather than the nitty-gritty of performing. Having spent most of Saturday morning blocking the moves of the first half of the show, and the rest of the afternoon going through musical numbers, then on Monday blocking the second half in the morning, with more music rehearsal in the afternoon, I was surprised on Tuesday morning when David Roden suddenly announced that he wanted a run-through of the show without scripts after lunch. I couldn't believe I'd heard right and approached him. I pointed out that we hadn't worked on any of the scenes yet, we had only just finished blocking it, and if we attempted a run-through at this stage, it would be a pointless shambles. But he was adamant.

Following one of the most fragmented rehearsals I've ever had the misfortune to attend, Roden sat the cast in the auditorium to give us notes and told us how bad we all were. I wasn't having any of that and pointed out that I told him it would be shambolic if he had a run-through at this stage. Glyn Kerslake, playing the Beast and Prince, had recently played the Phantom in *Phantom of the Opera* in the West End, and Terry Molly as the villain King Caliban, a regular Milkman character in *The Archers* for many years and Davros in *Dr Who,* and Mark Hayden as Muddles, who produced his own Murder Mystery Shows, all backed me up and agreed we should never have had a run-through. The director, feeling outnumbered, burst into tears and ran from the rehearsal.

While I sympathised that Malcolm's death may have had something to do with his emotional outburst, I suspected most of it was insecurity, knowing he was out of his depth as a director. This was his second in-house pantomime, and Malcolm had been his co-director the previous year, and I think it was probably Malcolm who set the correct agenda for the rehearsal period a year ago.

We managed to get the show up and running, despite Roden's often tearful exits from rehearsals when we seriously disagreed with him. We nicknamed him the 'rodent' and as we prepared to go on stage one night, he burst into our dressing room and accused us of running him down. Our radio mics had been switched on, and he had been eavesdropping in the sound man's booth.

Well, we all agreed, if you listen at keyholes, you only have yourself to blame.

Johnny McGee, who played the Chamberlain in the show, was an old friend of Malcolm's. He was a stand-up comedian and also ran his own business, supplying bouncers to West End clubs. He offered to take us clubbing one night.

After a Friday night show, Mark, Terry, Fiona Bruce (not the newsreader) who played Fairy in the panto, and myself, climbed into his Jaguar and he drove us into the West End. I can't remember the name of the first club we visited. There were many villains in attendance as earlier in the evening a boxing match had taken place there to celebrate some villain's release from a stretch inside. Johnny introduced us to two East End gangsters, Joey Pyle and Tony Lambrianou. Pyle was one of the biggest villains in London, running everything from protection rackets to drugs dealing. He was friends with the Krays and also with Charlie Richardson, the notorious south London mobster. And Tony Lambrianou was an enforcer for the Krays and spent fifteen years in jail for the murder of Jack 'the Hat' McVitie, although he denied knowing Ronnie was going to stab him. He did, however, dispose of the body.

When Pyle was introduced to Terry Molly and was told who he was, he said, 'You was Davros in *Dr Who?* You used to scare the shit out of me.'

Most gangsters usually manage to get publishing deals as they age. So it came as no surprise when I earwigged this conversation between Lambrianou's wife and Fiona.

'What does your husband do?'

'He's a writer.'

'What sort of things does he write?'

'Crime.'

'Does he know a lot about crime then?'

'Yeah.'

When I visited the toilet in this club, and happened to be standing at the urinal, I heard sniffing sounds. When I glanced over my shoulder I saw a long line of men stooped over a window ledge with twenty pound notes stuck up their noses, and I knew I had stumbled on a strange ritual, a curious club custom.

The next club Johnny took us to was Stringfellows. Call me naïve but I knew nothing about the club and imagined somewhere more upmarket than this rather tacky gilt, mirrors and chandeliers room, with faux zebra-skin chairs, and large-breasted topless lap dancers plying their trade. I watched, probably open-mouthed, as a well-heeled hooray-henry peeled off twenty-pound notes for his two lap dancers and topped up their champagne glasses, spending money like it came from a Monopoly set.

We didn't stay long at Stringfellows and were then taken to China White, more opulent and exclusive. Having driven from Chesham after the evening show, then visited the first two clubs, by now we were into the wee small hours. We were shown to a private room at China White and had been there perhaps an hour or two when there was an almighty rumpus in the bar, and Johnny asked his head doorman to get us out through the fire exit. He then took us to a small drinking club he co-owned just off Golden Square.

Later on, his doorman came over and told us what the altercation was about. Apparently, Bill Clinton's nephew or cousin was there with the ex-president's daughter, and there had been an argument and someone had stubbed a cigar out on his face, mistaking it for an ashtray.

After an exhausting and eventful night, I got back to my Chesham digs at six a.m. and crawled into bed, setting the alarm for 11.30. We had a matinee at one p.m. and I wondered how we could inject life into that run-of-the-mill show. I suppose we managed it, but my memory is fogged from a night out on the town.

I can remember, though, buying a copy of the *Evening Standard* between the matinee and evening show, and there was a picture of Chelsea Clinton exiting China White in an inebriated state. Johnny told us some time later that Clinton had been giving a speech at Oxford University that night, and planned on joining his daughter at the club, but was told by his secret service minders to abandon his visit because of the kerfuffle.

One of my close friends, Harry Lawson, who I met at the White Hart pub when I moved to Rusthall, came to see *Beauty and the Beast* along with his wife Bee, accompanied by Ken and Marion Thomson who owned the pub, and we arranged to go for a meal after the performance. Mark Hayden told me he was all alone after the show and could he join us for dinner afterwards. When I asked my friends from Rusthall if someone in the cast could join us for dinner, they said they didn't mind.

When we sat down and ordered our meal at a Chinese restaurant, Mark took out his mobile phone and proceeded to have a long conversation in front of us. And when Bee took out a packet of cigarettes, rather than interrupt his phone conversation, he clicked his fingers, indicating that he wanted one. Later on, she told me she couldn't quite believe how she obligingly handed one over. Not only that, she lit it for him as well. Meanwhile, Ken was getting hot under the collar and was about to grab the ill-mannered Muddles round the throat but Marion kept kicking him under the table. She said she didn't want Ken to ruin my evening.

Back in the White Hart after the panto ended, they told me that during the interval they had talked about their agreeing to someone in the cast joining us for dinner, wondered who it could be, and hoped it wasn't that bloke playing Muddles. There was just something about him…

And how right they were. But for a long while we all dined out on the story of the ill-mannered Muddles and the way Bee obligingly lit his cigarette for him.

For some time I had been trying to write about William Sutton, a real life bank robber from New York, set during the Prohibition era. It required a great deal of research, although I intended fictionalising it. In February 2002 I got in touch with an old stage school friend, Barry Halliday, who lives in New York City, and he invited me over to stay with him and his wife, so that I could get a real feel for the city, and he even drove me to Ossining in upstate New York so that I could visit Sing Sing Penitentiary, one of the prisons where Sutton was incarcerated for many years.

As soon as I arrived home in Rusthall, I knuckled down and began writing it, in between unusual though lucrative occasional employment, working for public organisations like the Department of Trade and Industry, writing and performing scenarios about diversity issues. It was Peter Cleall who fixed me up with this work, as Pelham Associates was no longer a co-operative agency and was run by Peter and his wife, actress Dione Inman, both of whom had changed careers and become full-time agents.

Then, starting in the late summer of 2007, I worked as a Writer in Residence in Aberdeen for a year, which was when my novel about William Sutton, *Willie the Actor*, was published.

During my time in Aberdeen I began writing a children's book, *The Ice Cream Time Machine*, which was published in 2009 by Andrews UK.

That year Peter Cleall phoned me with the bad news that Peter Denyer had died. Peter had lived for many years in Cheltenham and was prolific in writing pantomimes for Kevin Wood Productions, churning several out each year, and he often appeared in one of them, usually as the baddie. Apparently he collapsed while he was on his way to Cheltenham station. I was glad I had at least met with Peter once more when I was on the *Funny Money* tour in 1998 when we had lunch together at a pub in Cheltenham, not far from the Malvern Festival Theatre where I was performing.

I belong to the writers' trade union, The Writers' Guild of Great Britain, and at many meetings and events I met another writer, Adrienne Conway, who in the 1980s wrote two series of *Streets Apart,* a sitcom starring James Hazeldine and Amanda Redman. She now lived in Spain, and we kept in touch by phone or email. She kept inviting me to visit her, and it wasn't until 2011 that I decided to take her up on it, and booked a flight to Malaga, caught the airport bus to Marbella, where she picked me up and drove me to her flat in Estepona, further along the coast.

No sooner had we walked through the door than the television was switched on as she never missed an episode of *EastEnders*. All this way, I thought, and here I am forced to watch a soap I've never seen before and have no intention of watching in the future. Not that I have anything against it as such, but I am an avid reader and can't imagine reading a book in the same setting with the same characters in volume after volume ad infinitum. Surely there has to be an end somewhere?

I think my end came when over dinner later on I happened to pour myself a second glass of wine, and my host said, 'You drink a lot, don't you?'

I have four nights of this to get through, I can remember thinking. *This is worse than being married.*

In fairness to her, being a guest in someone's home is not the easiest way to get to know a person, especially when you early on discover you have little in common, other than the fact that you both happen to be writers. But there was worse to come.

She had adopted a stray cat, which feared strangers. Her bedroom had an en suite bathroom, and so did the guest bedroom, where she had placed the cat's litter tray, telling me not to shut the door, in case the cat needed to go in the night. She called it in for the night after I had gone to bed, because the cat was too scared to come anywhere near me. The next morning, I heard a yell, and then as I took a deep breath I was overwhelmed by the most disgusting reek of diarrhoea. The cat had shit in her wardrobe, and she accused me of shutting my bathroom door, depriving it of access to its litter tray. But I hadn't. It was because the cat was too scared to venture near me, took the easy way out, and did its business in some comfy clothing and shoes at the bottom of her wardrobe.

This event triggered the end for me, and I still had the third and final day to get through before my flight home. I was relieved when she suggested I spend the day in Marbella because she had some work to catch up on. I caught the bus to Marbella and had the best time of the entire trip, sitting in a café in the old town, drinking beer with a light tapas lunch, exploring the harbour, and seeing all the Salvador Dali statues dotting the quayside.

That night, back from my great solo day at Marbella, I took Adrienne for a Chinese meal to thank her for – er – introducing me to the one episode of *EastEnders* I had ever seen up until then. As I ordered a second glass of wine for myself, again she said, 'You drink a lot, don't you?'

I pointed out that as she used to be an actress, she must have worked with actors who drank a lot more. She told me all the actors she had worked with didn't drink much.

I wanted to say, 'You can't have worked much then.' But I hushed my mouth.

My flight from Malaga was at 3.15 in the afternoon, and at 10.30 I suggested we might leave, just in case the airport bus from Marbella was delayed. I arrived at the airport with three hours to spare before the flight, and it was my best airport experience ever, sitting in an airport bar enjoying a drink. I almost expected the barmaid to say, 'You drink a lot, don't you?'

Another visit to Spain in October, but this was relaxing and fun, staying with people I knew and loved. It was my second visit to see Carol Hawkins and her husband Martyn. I flew from Gatwick with our friends Mark Andrews and Henry Holland, and during the visit we never stopped laughing. When I related my tale of the earlier trip to Spain, everyone fell about. Especially the story about the cat shitting in the wardrobe. And as we sat by the pool, every time I poured myself another glass of wine, Carol said jokingly, 'You drink a lot, don't you?'

Self Isolation

2014 was to be an eventful year and something of a game changer. My first crime novel, *Each Man Kills,* published in Wales by Gomer Press in 2002, was now out of print, and the publisher Andrews UK agreed to reissue it, and also published another two books of mine, *Tales from Soho*, a book of short stories, and *A Deadly Diversion,* another crime novel.

One day, speaking on the telephone to Brian Murphy's wife Linda Regan, who played April in the *Hi-de-Hi* series and is also a crime novelist, she suggested I get in touch with Stuart Morriss at the Misty Moon Film Society. I met him and his wife Jen at a pub in Tunbridge Wells, and they then booked me to give a talk about my career at a café bar in Soho in August. This seemed to go down well, and when I met Stuart and his wife weeks later, he told me that although my talk had gone down well, the audience would have liked me to have done a bit of Frankie Abbott. I said as I was now in my seventies it might be embarrassing behaving like that juvenile blockhead. But suddenly I was hit by an idea. Why not play the character in real time, and write a play with Frankie Abbott now resident in an old people's home? I set about writing it, and as soon as it was complete, Stuart began finding venues in which to perform it, and Linda agreed to play the part of Marion, the carer in Frankie's residential home.

Because I was fortunate enough to get three books published by Andrews UK that year, I tried to get as many interviews with BBC local radio stations as possible. And around the same time I heard about a digital independent radio station broadcasting from Kent, and with a view to getting more publicity for my book I contacted them by email.

I received a reply from Kevin Cann, presenter, producer and co-owner of Channel Radio, who invited me to be interviewed on his show. Following the interview, Kevin, who loved the *Please Sir!* film, took me to lunch at a bistro next door to the Dymchurch studio and asked if I would be interested in presenting my own radio show.

Up until then I had never thought of myself as a radio presenter. But why not? I thought. And I broadcast my first show on Saturday 18 October of that year. It was Kevin who twiddled all the knobs and pressed all the buttons, and it was he who suggested I call it the Imaginarium Show and he also become producer of all my shows. To begin with, I just talked and told theatrical stories in between tracks. My first guest on the show was Marie Kelly, an actress and singer I had worked with for Katapult Productions, a cooperative production company I belonged to when we produced a play of mine called *A Friend of Ronnie's* about the train driver who was recruited by Ronnie Biggs to drive the train during the Great Train Robbery, and the script was later published by Lazy Bee Scripts, and has been performed by several amateur drama companies. Marie also took over as Marion for two performances of *A Day in The Lives of Frankie Abbott* in Luton and London, in which she was excellent, gave a very sensitive performance and was also very funny.

Later that year, Kevin instructed me in the technical features of the radio console so that I gradually began to operate the show myself.

***

I was saddened when I heard of the death of my old friend Richard Davies. Dickie had been in a home suffering from dementia for more than four years, and I attended his funeral at St Mary's Church, Bramshott, near Liphook in Hampshire, in late October. Six months later they held a memorial service for him at the Actors' Church, St Paul's in Covent Garden, and I was asked by Dickie and Jill's daughter, Nerissa Jory, to give a reading from *Under Milk Wood*. I went along with Stuart for the service, and also attending the service were Peter Cleall and Ray Brooks who was a close friend of Dickie and Jill. Peter knew Ray, having worked with him on television in *Big Deal* and *Growing Pains*. Following a tribute video, showing clips of Dickie in *Zulu, Please Sir!, Coronation Street and Fawlty Towers*, I got up and began to read the Reverend Eli Jenkins' morning prayer from a folder. I didn't notice the large candle beneath the lectern at which I stood until I heard a cry of alarm and someone rushed forward to save it from catching fire.

After the service, and the Prayer and Blessing given by Reverend Simon Grigg, in an informal brief thanks, he added, 'And I would like to thank David Barry for almost burning down my church.'

I think Dickie would have expected an ex-5C pupil to burn something down!

I don't know whether I was amused or not by the huddle of professional autograph collectors outside the gates of the church. I call them 'professional autograph collectors' because these are the obsessive accumulators of signatures who turn up at the stage doors of theatres from Land's End to John O'Groats demanding autographs from actors in plays they rarely bother to see. And presumably they keep their eyes peeled for celebrity funerals and memorial services so that they might add precious autographs to their collections.

After signing their books, it was a relief to join Jill, her family and friends for a celebratory drink above a restaurant in Covent Garden.

***

Hoping that my writing in *A Day in the Lives of Frankie Abbott* did justice to the subject of dementia, even though it was primarily a comedy, we began rehearsing at the Cinema Museum in April. As Linda Regan was playing Marion, Brian Murphy came along for moral support, made a few invaluable suggestions, and jokingly referred to himself as the ASM as he made us coffee. We opened at Phoenix Artist Club in Charing Cross Road, then followed this with a succession of one-night stands at small venues in the south east.

Someone who saw one of these shows offered us a venue at the Edinburgh Fringe Festival. This was at the end of the first week in May and we thought this was leaving it late; the festival began the first week in August. But, although it was a risky venture, we were tempted, and Stuart set about crowd funding for it.

But, as anyone who has ever been to Edinburgh during that season will tell you, the most crippling expense is accommodation when every hotel, apartment, bedsit, caravan, or tent raise their prices. Some keen performers even resort to sleeping in dormitories (I kid you not).

I was lucky, however, because I was at an event at Elstree Studios, and Norman Eshley, who played Geoffrey Fourmile in *George and Mildred,* introduced me to Caroline Walker who lives in Edinburgh, and she offered me a very generous deal for our two weeks while performing at the Fringe Festival.

Linda didn't fancy the Edinburgh gig and we cast Anita Graham for the fortnight's run. I had worked with her in *Funny Money* and thought she would be great as Marion. To begin with at the New Town Theatre we played to one or two people a night, but gradually word got around and our audience slowly began to build. Stuart and Jen arrived a few days after us and Stuart took over operating the lights. One night he met Micky Flanagan who came with his family to see the show. Stuart had a word with him, and he said he really loved it.

With only three nights of performances left, we had a five star review in *Edinburgh Evening News*, which was a shame it came towards the end of the run, but still it was good to get a rave review. And we had been warned that most performers come away from Edinburgh without the shirt on their back, but we survived it – thanks mainly to the many people who contributed during the crowd funding.

In September Misty Moon, in conjunction with director Jason Read of Robo Films, shot a short film I had written, a spoof horror called *Frankula*, where Frankie Abbott escapes dreamlike from the care home into a spooky cemetery where he encounters three vampires played by Caroline Munro (my filmed dinner date back in 1974), Judy Matheson, who had appeared in horror features like *Lust for a Vampire,* and Emma Dark, a young director of horror films. These three vampires were assisted by the sinister Doctor Spritzer, played by Martin Rudman. And Fenella Fielding added a voice-over for the film. Fenella had been a guest on my Imaginarium Show, when I asked her to do that line from *Carry On Screaming,* 'Do you mind if I smoke?' which she was more than happy to do. She kind of purred as she spoke it and I instantly imagined Harry H Corbett's reaction in the classic film as she started to steam with lust on the chaise longue in front of him. Around the time I interviewed her in my radio show, she was appearing at the Phoenix Artist Club in Charing Cross Road, reading from her autobiography. Fenella died from a stroke in September 2018. She was 90 and admirably kept herself busy as a performer almost to the end.

Stuart persuaded me to write a sequel to *Frankula*, with him producing and Jason directing again, and so I wrote another comedy horror called *Bad Friday,* Stuart got together an excellent cast including Vera Day, who in the late '50s starred in many films and played George Cole's girlfriend in *Too Many Crooks;* Gary Shail who was Spider in *Quadrophenia;* Charlotte Mounter who featured in the film *Relentless*; and Emma Dark and Martin Rudman were again involved in the story of Frankie Abbott's Easter outing where he steals a little girl's Easter egg and is haunted by a knife wielding giant rabbit.

Dickie's wife Jill had suffered a stroke, and in 2017 she passed-away. Their daughter Nerissa invited me to attend the funeral at Bramshott in September and asked if I would read the First Voice opening speech from *Under Milk*

Wood. I felt really honoured in giving the reading, especially as I had worked with Jill and Dickie so many times in the Welsh play, and I treasured many fond memories of our time together.

Over the next few years Stuart and Jen of Misty Moon hosted quite a few events at the Cinema Museum, which is one of London's hidden gems. Tucked away just off a backstreet between the Elephant and Castle and Kennington, it used to be a workhouse in the Victorian era and was just one of several of these harrowing dwellings inhabited by Charlie Chaplin and his brother Sidney who suffered much hardship and poverty in their childhood. But as we all know, Chaplin's story was one of rags to riches, and he has made a stunning contribution to cinema's history. As does the Cinema Museum, which is a treasure trove of cinema memorabilia collected from all over Britain, and it even has a small cinema where they have a regular showing of classic films.

In 2018, Misty Moon presented the 50th anniversary of *Please Sir!* at the museum, first of all showing the film in the early evening. I was delighted when Phil Lancaster attended. He is a fellow Channel Radio presenter who broadcasts a show immediately after mine on Saturday at 2 p.m. A lovely bloke, Phil was the drummer with the band The Lower Third, when David Bowie played with them, and it was during that memorable year that the legendary singer changed his name from Jones to Bowie, and those early years are captured brilliantly in Phil's book *At The Birth of Bowie.*

Our 50th anniversary played to a good house at the Cinema Museum, and following some clips from both the series and film, most of the evening was taken up with the audience throwing questions at Peter Cleall, Penny Spencer and me; and Carol made a brief appearance on Skype from Spain, which was projected onto the large screen. I had John Alderton's email address, and had asked him if he would like to attend the reunion, but he declined, saying he had retired ten years ago, and never did retrospective interviews about his career, but invited Peter, Penny and me to have lunch with him, which was another lovely reunion when we had wine with him and Pauline Collins, and then he took us to a Greek restaurant for lunch, where we drank much wine – well, John and I did, as Peter and Penny don't drink alcohol anymore. But it was great to meet up and talk over old times.

The last five years presenting on Channel Radio have been a great comfort, and I have had many laughs during the times I spent broadcasting. I have interviewed many guests over the years, from Tom Baker, only my second guest in 2014 at the old Dymchurch studio, to Alan Clark, lead singer of the Hollies, interviewed more recently from the new studios in Ashford.

And then came the crunch in March this year. I was about to travel to Ashford for my Saturday show, when my guest was going to be Norman Eshley, but we were suddenly in lockdown and we couldn't go anywhere or do anything.

Also, not good timing for the release of my latest book, *Before They Die*, which was published on 19 March by Caffeine Nights Publishing. But hopefully, people have had more time on their hands recently, so you never know.

If anyone had predicted when we began *Please Sir!* in 1968 that it would be resuscitated in the twenty-first century, I would have thought they had a screw loose. But as I struggle with boredom during the lockdown, although I have spent much of the three months of isolation writing this memoir, I discover Forces TV are repeating the series, showing two episodes every weekday, twice a day. I watched the first episode of the second series, the one where I blow a raspberry coupled with a V-sign at Hedges in the opening credits and discovered that the rude gesture had been edited out. Why, I thought, was this regarded as politically incorrect? Maybe they were considering airmen, sailors and soldiers' sensibilities. Perhaps many squaddies would have been upset and shocked by this impertinent gesture.

But at least with the abundance of channels delving into the archives for material, I can enjoy watching many of my *Please Sir!* friends acting in various films and TV series. I had forgotten until I saw the Beatles' film *A Hard Day's Night* again recently, that Deryck Guyler played a police sergeant in it. One of the ITV channels has been running episodes of *The Sweeney* and I happened to catch an episode Malcolm McFee was in, playing Lukey Sparrow. And it was great to see Barbara Mitchell again when Talking Pictures repeated *For The Love of Ada*. Many of my Facebook friends mentioned they had seen me in an episode of *Never The Twain*. I have of course, like most of my *Fenn Street* counterparts, performed a variety of roles over the years, but it is *Please Sir!* which has had the biggest impact on my life, mainly because it resulted in the long-standing friendships that came about not only as a direct result of those halcyon days but also through other performance work relating to those sitcom years.

It also brought me a few repeats now and again, and a new and younger audience latched on to it, mainly through the film which has often been shown on Film 4; but more importantly the series brought me friendship, which came about as a direct result of the success of the series. Some of those friends have fallen by the wayside and sadly died much too young, but they still live on in my wonderful memories of the many years we enjoyed together and watching them again in the digital age is a great bonus. So just why was *Please Sir!* above and beyond everything else I did so important? Simply because what was once called *Rough House* back in 1968 is a conduit to what I value most in life:

Friendship.

Appendices

Appendix 1

Please Sir! 1971 Film Cast List

CHARACTER	PLAYED BY
Bernard Hedges	John Alderton
Norman Potter	Deryck Guyler
Mr. Cromwell	Noel Howlett
Doris Ewell	Joan Sanderson
Mr. Price	Richard Davies
Mr. Smith	Erik Chitty
Angela Cutforth	Patsy Rowlands
Eric Duffy	Peter Cleall
Sharon Eversleigh	Carol Hawkins
Maureen Bullock	Liz Gebhardt
Frankie Abbott	David Barry
Dennis Dunstable	Peter Denyer
Peter Craven	Malcolm McFee
Penny Wheeler	Jill Kerman
Mrs. Abbott	Barbara Mitchell
Mr. Dunstable	Peter Bayliss
Mrs. Duffy	Brenda Cowling
Mrs. Dunstable	Eve Pearce
Wesley	Brinsley Forde
Feisal	Aziz Resham
Reynolds	Norman Bird
Nobbler	Nicky Locise
Gypsy	Frederick Beauman
Old Gypsy Lady	Daphne Heard
Coach Driver	Jack Smethurst
Malcolm	Richard Everett
Parsons	Hayden Evans
Teacher	Gregory Scott
Kid	Graham Angell
Pupil	Jenny Irvine
Pupil	George Georghiou
Irate Hillman Driver	Tony Allen (uncredited)
Pupil	Richard Calder (uncredited)
Boy in Assembly	Todd Carty (uncredited)

Appendix 2

Please Sir! TV Episode List

Series 1

1. The Welcome Mat   First broadcast: 08.11.68
Newly qualified teacher Bernard Hedges doesn't make the best start to his post at Fenn Street; he's late, makes an immediate enemy of the belligerent caretaker Norman Potter, and is placed in charge of the notoriously terrible Form 5C...

2. A Picture of Innocence   First broadcast: 15.11.68
Mr Hedges encourages 5C to produce sketches for the school's art club. One in particular gets the other staff somewhat riled...

3. Maureen Bullock Loves Sir   First broadcast: 22.11.68
Following a study of *Romeo & Juliet*, Maureen reveals her affections for Mr Hedges. And when nosey Fenn Street neighbours see them together, a scandal develops and threatens Hedges' career as a teacher.

4. A Near Greek Tragedy   First broadcast: 29.11.68
When a troublesome Greek pupil returns to school for the first time during the term, having been detained on judicial matters, he resents Mr Hedges' attempts at discipline and calls in his tough uncle to sort him out.

5. Barbarian Librarians   First broadcast: 06.12.68
Tasked with looking after the school library, Mr Hedges ropes 5C in to help. When the room is ransacked, the staff know exactly where the blame lies.

6. Student Princess   First broadcast: 13.12.68
A new trainee teacher arrives at the school and turns out to be an old girlfriend of Bernard's. He's thrilled to be reunited with her, but soon feels threatened by the way she captivates his 5C class.

7. It's the Thought that Counts   First broadcast: 20.12.68
It's the last day of the Autumn term, and Bernard wonders if 5C will have got him a Christmas gift. Similarly, Potter and the headmaster are thrilled at the thoughts of a present from the rest of the staff. But 5C's previous teacher, Mr Wiggins, is due to return for the Spring term, and it starts to look as if Bernard will be parted from 5C.

Series 2

1. They're Off   First broadcast: 16.09.69

On the first day of term, a painter and decorator has yet to add the finishing touches to 5C's classroom, and Mr Hedges discovers his street-wise class are pretty good at fractions when it involves gambling.

2. Common Law   First broadcast: 23.09.69

On her way home from school, Sharon is almost attacked by a "dirty old man" on the common. Unfortunately for Potter, 5C decide to take the law into their own hands.

3. Panalal Passes By   First broadcast: 03.10.69

Bernard's attempts to restart the school's defunct Parent/Teacher Association has an outcome for which he is not prepared, and Potter becomes ever more exasperated when he discovers he has overdone the catering facilities.

4. The Sporting Life   First broadcast: 10.10.69

Bernard is coaxed into taking on the role of sports master, organising swimming outings and an inter-school boxing match, when he discover Duffy has an embarrassing secret.

5. Norman's Conquest   First broadcast: 17.10.69

Being encouraged at adopt a wild animal as a pet, 5C adopt a jerboa, which succeeds in annoying Potter.

6. X Certificate   First broadcast: 24.10.69

Fenn Street is having an open day and every class must participate, even 5C. The problem is that no-one told Bernard, who has to search for ideas during the last minute.

7. The Decent Thing   First broadcast: 31.10.69

Hungover after a session in the local pub, Hedges wakes up and finds himself in a strange woman's bed. Discovering that she is the mother of one of his pupils, he sinks into a state of confusion, especially when he hears that she's in the club!

8. The Generation Gap   First broadcast: 07.11.69

5C are, for once, making good use of their time in a community project. However, a rather recalcitrant pensioner refuses their offers of assistance, until Peter Craven is determined to get around him.

9. Life Without Doris   First broadcast: 14.11.69

When Miss Ewell entertains the notion of moving to Australia, Mr Price rather fancies stepping into her shoes as assistant headteacher, but his hopes for promotion are very soon dashed when Miss Ewell has other ideas.

10. The School Captain   First broadcast: 21.11.69

The Headmaster devises a school 'house' system but when 5C appoint their house captain it becomes a problem for Dunstable.

11. Out of the Frying Pan   First broadcast: 28.11.69

Staff and students alike no longer tolerate the appalling school dinners. But the Headmaster has a great appetite for them. Or so he believes...

12. Mixed Doubles   First broadcast: 05.12.69

After a raucous night out is had by the staff, and when Abbott is in trouble with the police, Bernard discovers that some members of the public are even more threatening than 5C.

13. Dress Circle   First broadcast: 12.12.69

The fifth form are heading to see a production of Romeo and Juliet at the theatre. Miss Ewell isn't too impressed with a number of revealing modern fashions displayed by 5C, and even Mr Hedges and Potter are for once united in their bid for individuality.

Short Insert. All Star Comedy Carnival   First broadcast: 25.12.69

Short festive special with the staff and pupils of Fenn Street Secondary Modern.

Series 3

1. Ag Bow Rumber   First broadcast: 20.09.70

A new term starts at Fenn Street, which means more problems for Bernard as this will be 5C's final term and he has to consider their future prospects, including his own when he meets the attractive Penny Wheeler.

2. Stitches & Hitches   First broadcast: 27.09.70

Bernard makes an unplanned spur-of-the-moment proposal to Penny while Abbott is hospitalised with appendicitis and overhears something he misinterprets.

3. Knick Knack Taffy Whack   First broadcast: 04.10.70

Mr Price, unnaturally cheery and amenable when the headmaster agrees to give him the following week off, arouses speculation with both staff and 5C pupils about where he is going. It soon becomes clear when form 5C watch television.

4. Enter Mister Sibley   First broadcast: 11.10.70

A career adviser, Mr Sibley, pays the school a visit: as does an army recruitment officer, at Potter's insistence. And Duffy discovers there is a cold harsh world outside of school.

5. It's a Saint Bernard's Life   First broadcast: 18.10.70

Smithy collapses in the street, and when Bernard visits him at home, he becomes smitten with this idyllic married life, but his fiancée Penny has more down-to-earth dreams.

6. Two and Two Make Nun   First broadcast: 25.10.70

Maureen feels rejected – not only by Sir, who steps in to try and stop her from becoming a nun, but also in turn by Monsignor Sopwith.

7. The Honour of the School   First broadcast: 01.11.70

Hedges is challenged to a game of golf. With the cheating help of 5C he wins, but the revelation of their deceit has repercussions for everyone, and there's money and a Majorcan holiday at stake!

8. Cromwell's Last Stand   First broadcast: 08.11.70

As 5C consider their future careers, Potter is yet again in trouble with a length of carpet that should be in the headmaster's study, and he has to make a deal with 5C.

9. Catch a Falling Drop-Out   First broadcast: 15.11.70

Attempting to teach 5C about politics, Mr Hedges arranges outings to the local Conservative and Labour clubs. But Maureen becomes a rebel and succeeds in causing trouble at the Conservative club.

10. A Star Is Born   First broadcast: 22.11.70

Surprising everyone, Potter is chosen as the model for a nationwide advertising campaign. But when the Head of Governors disapproves, he wonders if the situation can be rectified or is this the end of his career as school keeper?

11. The Facts of Life   First broadcast: 29.11.70

While decorating his new flat with Penny, Bernard is thrown into a moral quandary when Abbott reveals his ignorance about procreation. Does he correct Abbott and risk suspension from his job, or allow the fictions to remain unchallenged?

12. Situations Vacant   First broadcast: 06.12.70

As 5C prepare to enter the real world, Hedges worries about Dennis's lack of prospects. Can he help the boy find a position working close to the animals he loves? But Hedges soon discovers the biggest problem is in placating Dennis's bullying father.

13. Peace In Our Time   First broadcast: 13.12.70

On the last day of school 5C promise to behave for Hedges. But as Bernard attempts to 'play it cool', the kids begin to get the hump. Will they or won't they accept the invitations to his wedding to Penny?

14. And Everyone Came Too (*Xmas Special*) First broadcast: 27.12.70

It's the day of the wedding, and very little is running entirely to plan, but the guests are gathered, the couple are ready, and the show must go on! Fingers crossed from here on in...

Appendix 3

The Fenn Street Gang TV Episode List

Series 1

1. <u>Should Auld Acquaintance</u>　　　　First broadcast 17.09.71

No longer able to say 'Please, Sir' when they have a problem, the gang are now out in the cold world, but school friendships die hard and they are determined to keep their group identity.

2. <u>The Start of Something Big</u>　　　　First broadcast 24.09.71

Eric and Sharon encounter difficulties in their relationship, and the problems are compounded when ace 'tec' Frankie Abbott comes onto the scene.

3. <u>Leave it to Me, Darling</u>　　　　First broadcast 01.10.71

The Fenn Street Gang gets a new temporary member: their old class teacher Bernard Hedges.

4. <u>Horses for Courses</u>　　　　First broadcast 08.10.71

Maureen takes Dennis to a party and he soon discovers who his true friends are.

5. <u>Meet the Wizard</u>　　　　First broadcast 15.10.71

Penny, having decided a woman's place is not at home, tries to keep it secret from Bernard, who has a new job as a food demonstrator in a department store, which eventually brings him into contact with Abbott.

6. <u>Distant Horizons</u>　　　　First broadcast 22.10.71

When Sharon meets a student, Eric becomes extremely jealous, and their relationship is put to the test.

7. <u>Change Partners</u>　　　　First broadcast 29.10.71

Bernard Hedges, the bills piling up at home, wants to start work at university. When a friend suggests a lucrative part-time job, he jumps at the chance, leading to all kinds of complications.

8. <u>The Thin Yellow Line</u>　　　　First broadcast 05.11.71

When Abbott is forced to leave Archie Drew's detective agency a new career waits for him as a professional soldier. But even this becomes something of a disaster.

9. <u>All Mod Cons</u>　　　　First broadcast 12.11.71

Dennis has problems when he leaves home, and Eric also has difficulties when he enlists Peter Craven to help with a decorating job.

10. <u>These Foolish Things</u>   First broadcast 19.11.71

Abbott is in hospital with a stab wound, while Eric has another dust-up with Sharon, using Dennis's new flat as a rendezvous.

11. <u>Rough Justice</u>   First broadcast 26.11.71

When Dennis falls into bad company, it results in his appearance at a magistrate's court. But when Duffy and Craven appear for the defence, things go from bad to worse.

12. <u>Who Was That Lady?</u>   First broadcast 03.12.71

Duffy regrets breaking up with Sharon but is not averse to chatting up another girl, especially when her father can put some business his way.

13. <u>Kill or Cure</u>   First Broadcast 10.12.71

Waiting for her 'O' level results Maureen is on edge, results which will help her nursing career. What better cure for her nerves than a date with a nice chap, but not when that chap is picked by Duffy and Craven.

14. <u>When Did You Last See Your Father?</u>   First broadcast 24.12.71

Jealous of Craven's new gift, Abbott commits a crime and is put on probation, and his mother tells him lies, further indulging his fantasies.

15. <u>A Fair Swap</u>   First broadcast 31.12.71

The gang are involved in a medical rag week, and it becomes complicated when Maureen is kidnapped with the assistance of Frankie 'Nurse' Abbott.

16. <u>The Clean Weekend</u>   First broadcast 01.01.72

When the gang decide to have a day out at the seaside, Eric and Sharon decide to stay the night at a hotel, getting them into all kinds of trouble.

17. <u>Tally Ho!</u>   First broadcast 14.01.72

Dennis Dunstable tries to get his father to see sense and turn over a new leaf with the assistance of Peter Craven

18. <u>Horse of the Year</u>   First broadcast 21.01.72

Dennis has to decide how to spend his birthday money, and the gang attend an auction.

19. <u>From Sudbury With Love</u>   First broadcast 28.01.72

Frankie Abbott has a night out on the town where he hopes to find himself a girlfriend, then discovers almost too late that he is being pressured into marriage.

20. <u>Who's Minding the Shop?</u>   First broadcast 04.02.72

The gang unintentionally become shopkeepers, and it happens because of an accident.

21. <u>The Great Frock Robbers</u>   First broadcast 11.02.72

Sharon's job at the boutique is compromised when she is blamed for not spotting a gang of thieves. Part of the problem was in giving Frankie the job of store detective.

Series 2

1. <u>The Crunch</u>   First broadcast 15.10.72

As Duffy attempts to run his small family business, he soon discovers how difficult it can be and the sacrifices he has to make in order to survive.

2. <u>Smart Lad Wanted</u>   First broadcast 22.10.72

When Craven is out of work, Bowler, a local villain offers him employment, and Abbott also becomes involved. Duffy warns Craven not to get mixed up in anything dodgy but he doesn't heed his advice.

3. <u>The Woman for Dennis</u>   First broadcast 29.10.72

The gang are pleased when Dennis announces that he has found a girlfriend. But when they meet her they discover she is almost old enough to be his mother, so they decide to clip Cupid's wings.

4. <u>Menagerie a Trois</u>   First broadcast 05.11.72

Mrs Abbott takes in a lodger and a romance develops between them. Frankie is seething with jealousy and moves in with Dennis. But Abbott and his mother deserve each other too much for the parting to be permanent.

5. <u>That Sort of Girl</u>   First broadcast 12.11.72

As he endeavours to stay in business, Duffy struggles to find the money to pay for some new ladders, Sharon offers to help by entering a beauty contest. But Duffy has strong views on beauty contests.

6. <u>The Left Hand Path</u>   First broadcast 19.11.72

Working for the villainous Bowler has brought Craven flash clothes and a car, and cannot resist showing them off to Duffy, who is struggling financially. But showing off with Bowler's money is not only daft but could be dangerous.

7. <u>The Lady with the Lamp</u>   First broadcast 26.11.72

Having passed her exams, Maureen begins a nursing career. Unfortunately for some of her patients and nursing staff, her over-the-top enthusiasm makes them wonder if they have met a modern-day Florence Nightingale.

8. <u>The Loneliest Night of the Week</u>   First broadcast 03.12.72

Finding contact with the opposite sex difficult, Dennis and Frankie, taking advice from Peter and Sharon, enrol for dancing lessons to see if they can make some friends. Frankie has other ideas which get him into hot water.

9. <u>Father's Day</u>   First broadcast 10.12.72

Mr Dunstable, having had a drunken row with his wife, decides to move in with Dennis. But Dennis, who is now making slow progress with a girlfriend, has other ideas.

10. Low Noon   First broadcast 17.12.72

Mr Bowler likes Peter Craven's 'style', but also thinks Duffy has style and wants him on his payroll. But when Duffy turns him down, Bowler thinks anyone's mind can be changed – with a little persuasion.

11. And Baby Makes Three   First broadcast 31.12.72

Craven gets himself a bachelor pad, then gives a lift to a heavily pregnant hitch-hiker, and his love nest soon begins to look like a nursing home.

12. Is That a Proposal, Eric?   First broadcast 07.01.73

Sharon has been Eric Duffy's girlfriend since they were at Fenn Street School. And begins to think she will still only be his girlfriend when they are drawing their pensions, which leads her to take drastic steps to change the course of their future together.

13. Private Eye and Public Nuisance   First broadcast 14.01.73

Mrs Abbott meets private investigator Archie Drew and persuades him to re-employ Frankie, who now enjoys life on the dole, spending all his days in bed, waking occasionally to play with his new camera.

14. Dypsomania on Sea   First broadcast 21.01.73

When Dennis is persuaded to take a holiday by the sea, his father goes too and attempts to take the cure. But when the sea air revives the spirits of both father and son, elderly residents at the hotel are horrified at their behaviour.

15. Is Anybody There?   First broadcast 28.01.73

Maureen gets the gang interested in spiritualism, and they attend a meeting held by Mr Grout, a medium who hints that one of them could easily turn out to be a medium too. Abbott immediately assumes he has psychic powers.

16. How to Handle a Woman   First broadcast 04.02.73

Craven resents the way his mother henpecks his father, so decides to incite his father to rebel. And he succeeds – in splitting them up!

17. Business Deficiency   First broadcast 11.02.73

The writing is on the wall for Eric's painting and decorating business, so he decides that what is needed is to invest in a new business model and to put it on a more formal footing.

18. Absent Friends   First broadcast 18.02.73

Eric and Sharon's engagement becomes official and they have a party to celebrate. What better time than now for the happy couple to have all their old school friends around them? Or is it? Is the planned party courting disaster?

Series 3

1. An Englishman's Home   First broadcast 27.05.73

Now they are engaged, Duffy and Sharon start looking for a home of their own. They think they have found somewhere until Frankie Abbott loses them the chance to buy it. And their problems are compounded when he tries to make amends.

2. Mother Knows Best   First broadcast 03.06.73

Frankie makes the terrible mistake of taking his girlfriend Celeste home to meet his mother and hasn't reckoned on how difficult the confrontation will become.

3. Alone At Last   First broadcast 10.06.73

Wedding bells finally ring for Duffy and Sharon and after all the logistical problems have been ironed out, the happy couple just want to be alone. But fate has a habit of intervening.

4. After the Ball   First broadcast 24.06.73

Craven has been walking the tightrope for far too long and it is the idiot Frankie that makes him lose his balance. But can Duffy provide him with a safety net?

5. The Ant and the Grasshopper   First broadcast 01/07/73

Duffy has taken on Craven as an assistant painter in his business but their relationship is soon put under strain. Something has to give, and it soon looks as if it will lead to an increase in the unemployment figures.

7. Abbott of Arabia   First broadcast 08.07.73

Mrs Abbott goes too far in her high-handed ways of dealing with Frankie. It changes him into a fantasy 'Red Shadow' and he gallops off with Celeste to the Registry Office.

8. Full Circle   First broadcast 15.07.73

Sharon has a little secret. Unfortunately, it becomes somewhat difficult to share with Eric when they are not even talking.

About the Author

David Barry began his professional acting career at just twelve years old and would go on to perform alongside such luminaries as Sir Laurence Olivier, Vivien Leigh and Paul Scofield. Many fans fondly remember him as Frankie Abbott from the LWT sitcoms *Please, Sir!* and *The Fenn Street Gang*, a role he greatly enjoyed playing. David is also a stalwart of the pantomime scene, having appeared in over thirty shows in a variety of roles from Buttons to Dame. He has continued acting throughout his long career, appearing in everything from episodes of *The Bill* to spoof horror films *Frankula* and *Bad Friday* which can both be seen on YouTube. Even at the start of his career David showed an interest in writing, with his first credit being an episode of *The Fenn Street Gang*. He would later work on the classic Thames TV sitcom *Keep It in the Family*, lend his skills to the public sector as a training video scriptwriter, and write material for himself to perform in *Radio Fun*, a stage show he took on tour in the 1990s. As a novelist David has written six crime thrillers, a children's book and the historical novel *Mr Micawber Down Under*. Returning to play perhaps his most famous role, he brought *A Day in the Lives of Frankie Abbott* to the 2016 Edinburgh Fringe, receiving 5-star reviews across the board. David lives in Tunbridge Wells and has two grown-up children.

Index

David Barry is the author of...

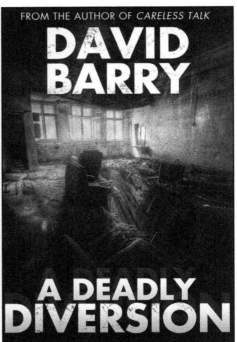

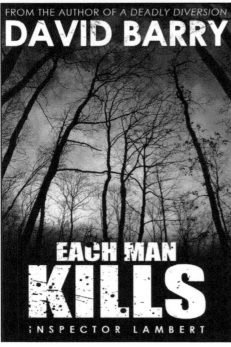

Lightning Source UK Ltd.
Milton Keynes UK
UKHW020431011220
374381UK00001B/22